To Sylvia,
From April xxx
March 2008

Little Laureates

Hertfordshire Poets

Edited by Claire Tupholme

First published in Great Britain in 2008 by:
Young Writers
Remus House
Coltsfoot Drive
Peterborough
PE2 9JX
Telephone: 01733 890066
Website: www.youngwriters.co.uk

SB ISBN 978-1 84431 431 7

Foreword

Young Writers was established in 1991 and has been passionately devoted to the promotion of reading and writing in children and young adults ever since. The quest continues today. Young Writers remains as committed to the nurturing of poetic and literary talent as ever.

This year's Young Writers competition has proven as vibrant and dynamic as ever and we are delighted to present a showcase of the best poetry from across the UK and in some cases overseas. Each poem has been selected from a wealth of *Little Laureates* entries before ultimately being published in this, our sixteenth primary school poetry series.

Once again, we have been supremely impressed by the overall quality of the entries we have received. The imagination, energy and creativity which has gone into each young writer's entry made choosing the poems a challenging and often difficult but ultimately hugely rewarding task - the general high standard of the work submitted ensured this opportunity to bring their poetry to a larger appreciative audience.

We sincerely hope you are pleased with this final collection and that you will enjoy *Little Laureates Hertfordshire Poets* for many years to come.

Contents

Chorleywood Primary School

The Poems

Vampires

The vampire burns down the people,
Under a full, spooky moon.
He brings another vampire and another and another,
They have a lot of fun.
The humans screaming bursting out their blood!
The blood makes a river into a sea.

Vampires still hungry,
Went down to the town,
Looking for people,
With their bloody eyes.

The people crying from the pain
And running into their houses.
Vampire says evilly, 'We can still catch you, ha, ha, ha.'
They burst into your house
And suck your blood out.
Vampires evil, humans poor.
Dogs bark and got their eyeballs.

One day later, the bones crunching,
Still there is a river of blood.

Ben Kim (11)

Dunstable Downs

I want to be at Dunstable Downs
Windy, blowy and cold
I want to be where the ground
Meets with the misty, cold weather
I want to be where coloured kites
Are flying in the blue
I want to be at Dunstable Downs
Windy, blowy and cold.

Jemima Wesson (10)
Abbots Langley School

The Sea

The sea is as rough as my hair in the morning,
As blue as the sky.
The sea sways to and fro,
Smashes onto the rocks.
The sea makes ripples of waves from the wind,
Is as cold as the snow.
The sea is as blue as bright blue eyes,
Is crystal clear and seaweed glistens.
The waves are like a shooting star,
As they ripple across the surface.
The sea glows like an evening sunset,
Is as light as a feather.
The sea waves are as high as bouncing on a trampoline,
As pretty as a snowy day.
The sea is as sparkly as the moon and the stars.
The waves are as sharp as a roller coaster.
The sea is . . .

Isabel King (10)
Abbots Langley School

The Stormy Sea

I was at the sea
Standing . . .
On a rock and the sea
Came smashing, dashing and crashing
Like horses charging, hitting me
Like I was in a war.

I was at the sea
Crouching . . .
On a rock and the sea
Came smashing, dashing and crashing
Enormously high
Like an elephant standing on two legs
Hitting me like a tornado.

Aaron Routley (10)
Abbots Langley School

Down In The Forest

Down in the forest where nobody goes,
There's a great big lake with flowers all around,
It shimmers and it glimmers and it sparkles in the light,
Down in the forest where nobody goes.

Down in the forest where nobody goes,
There are hills and valleys, rocky and green,
You can taste the air, warm but it stops your heart,
The moss is furry, but a beauty too,
Down in the forest where nobody goes.

Down in the forest where nobody goes,
The trees are elegant and bristly too,
They're tall and thick, you can't see the top,
The snakes are hissing and the trees are whistling,
Down in the forest where nobody goes.

Devon Prior (11)
Abbots Langley School

Volcano

The size of a skyscraper,
Taller than the clouds,
Huge compared to a butterfly,
But not bigger than the world.
Out comes lava,
Bursting out with fury,
Pointing to the sky,
With rocks,
Jagged on the ground . . .

The size of an enormous rocket,
Taller than the clouds,
Huge compared to a person,
Lovely to be a photographer,
Interested by its magnificence . . .

Levi Woolley (10)
Abbots Langley School

Mountain

The breathtaking Rocky Mountains
Are windy and dangerous
The top is jagged and cold
Icy and rough
Step by step
It gets steeper and steeper
The air is fresh
The rocks are slippery
Outstanding and high
Rocks are tumbling
And clashing
Smaller than an ant
My bones
Are shaking with fear
I can smell the moss on the rocks
I can feel the sharp rocks
I'm at the top
I can see
Everything is possible . . .

Sam Wood (10)
Abbots Langley School

The Volcano

The volcano is so hot under our feet
You feel like an oven
The volcano is so hard
Like nothing can destroy it
The volcano is hot
Boiling and rough
Like a rhino
The volcano is
Like an earthquake.

Brandon Tyrell (10)
Abbots Langley School

The Fast-Flowing River

The fast-flowing river
Like a rocket floating
To the dark sky
It rushes downhill
It sprays its glistening cold
You look at the water
You are the one floating
Down river . . .

As the river meets the edge
It crashes
Down on the water below
Sounds like balls
Splashing into baths
But ten times bigger
As the water
In the fast-flowing river
Collides with the riverbanks
The water flies
Like a newborn bird.

Alex Spratt (10)
Abbots Langley School

Vesuvius

I went down to Vesuvius
When the volcano erupted
Lava spreading
Like a wild stream
Rocks flying like an army
The taste . . . hot as it hit my tongue
The smell . . . of rock burning
The sound . . . of a lion roaring
I went down to Vesuvius
And I saw the most beautiful sight
But with it was also a terrible might.

Amelie Gregory (10)
Abbots Langley School

Where The Sea Meets The Rocks

When I watch
The magnificent sea
I think forever of home
Where the seagulls swoop
And the cliffs stand tall
Shading the ground
And the sea meets the rocks
With an almighty clash
Clash
Clash
The sea meets the rocks
With an almighty clash . . .

Oh, mighty sea
With thrashing waves
Attacking the small boat
Then a sudden sound
Of crumbling wood
The sea takes the lives of many
And the sea meets the rocks
With an almighty clash
Clash
Clash
The sea meets the rocks
With an almighty clash . . .

Emily Cooke (10)
Abbots Langley School

Mount Everest

It sent a mighty shiver down my spine
I looked at the towering castle
Intrigued by its magnificence
It changed my perfect heartbeat
I realised
I was miniscule
Compared to the immense
Mount Everest
My bright blue eyes
On my pale white face
Widened
At the jagged mountain ahead.

Another step is way too far
But a step back is not good enough
Higher than a crisp, golden leaf
But lower than the clouds
Intrigued by its magnificence
Although thou death threat of my life
I walked away
Scared out of this world
I turned back to the crooked Mount Everest
And said my last goodbye.

Isabelle Minihan (10)
Abbots Langley School

The Storm

The waves were rough
Crashed and splashed
Huge and high
And so amazing!
A massive storm!

Sharp rocks
Pointed on the end
Rocky, slippery
And crumbling
Down to the bottom of the sea
I could see them falling

My boat collided
The rocks smashed
I was swimming
In the sea
Screaming
Then I saw it
An outstanding, massive wave
It took me under
I stayed under.

Molly Ambler (10)
Abbots Langley School

The Wind

The mighty storm destroys our world
Everything in sight
Dawn, sunrise
The next day calms us
With its gentle breeze
This beautiful thing entertains us
Especially on sunny days
The wind is our friend
Wind is our trust.

Alexander Winfield (10)
Abbots Langley School

The River

The river
Gushes and splashes,
As it spills over the waterfall
Crashes below,
Chucking
Heavy waves,
The waterfall
Cascading down,
Tall as a mighty giant,
Loud as a lion's roar.

The river
Trickles round,
With the glistening water
See the magnificent waterfall
From miles away,
Frantically streams down
Like a slippery snake.
Hard to stand up,
Tall as a mighty giant,
Loud as a lion's roar.

Alice Drake (10)
Abbots Langley School

The Mountain

The mountain is very steep
And also chucks down with loads of snow
The size of a lighthouse.
Also a big, sharp point
Very, very shiny like a star.

The mountain very tall
The snow chucks down very hard
With millions of snow
A brilliant triangle at the top
Shiny like a glistening sun.

Harry Smith (10)
Abbots Langley School

Cheddar Gorge

The crumbling rock,
Tumbles down,
Smashing through the sides of the gorge,
Slowly sculpting the vast and twisted walls,
Of the ever widening basin.

The towering walls,
Concealed by rocks,
Reflecting each other,
Imprisoning all who step within,
The mouth of this towering mountain.

This mountainous valley,
Carved from stone,
Will soon become,
Just a pile of dust.

Scott Denton (10)
Abbots Langley School

Mighty Mountains

A mountain . . . a mighty pyramid
Made out of rock.
The thrill of rushing towards a monstrous rocket,
Bigger than anything you could ever dream of.
Powdery snow on the tips of icy granite,
A dangerous rock,
Jagged at the edges.
Almighty mountains,
Frown down at you
From their outstanding height,
To tip down like a deep basin.
Spectacular views are . . .
The long awaited prizes
Climbing up a steep mountain.

Emma Kingsley (10)
Abbots Langley School

Water Valley

The sparkling lake
Shines over the valley
The icy winds
Blow all around me
The rocky waterfall
Crashes down
Into the spring
The fresh air slowly whispers past me
And the spectacular stars
Sparkle over the valley . . .

The sparkling moon
Up high with the stars
Shines onto the valley
The waterfall slowly splashes
Into the lake
The spring is calm and smooth
While the fresh, moany wind
Brushes past me.

Tom Jeffries (10)
Abbots Langley School

The River

A bubbling river
As calm as the clouds
Full of the colours of the rainbow
A slithering snake
That wanders through the woods
At night with caution

And as light as a feather
The stars from the heavens above
Shine their little bright light on the river
Like a stream of lights
That make a path of magic.

Tempany Mapp (11)
Abbots Langley School

Panclear Valley

Dry moss crumbles underfoot,
The twang of a bow,
Twigs snap like panthers' jaws,
The sloshing of foamy waves,
Steam rises off the cascading falls,
Nearby the Beor Mountains,
Tower like mighty giants.

The sight of apple-green grass,
Welcoming you to the rolling hills,
The feel of rough bark,
Crumbling beneath nimble fingers,
The smell of the trickling salty waves,
And . . . nearby the Beor Mountains,
Tower like mighty giants.

The roar of the cascading waves,
A great lion tumbling down,
Lake Cleo, sparkling, a star,
Slow and gentle as mother to infant,
Shrill bird calls, just awoken from slumber,
And . . . nearby the Beor Mountains,
Tower like mighty giants.

April Turner (10)
Abbots Langley School

Autumn

A nimals getting ready for hibernation
U nder the leaves you will find the hedgehogs
T ons of leaves floating through the air
U p in the trees squirrels chase each other
M oonlight reflects off the shining lake
N aughty foxes chasing rabbits.
Hibernation time!

Taylor Roberts (11) & Maisy Plater (10)
Aldbury Primary School

Midnight Moon

Midnight moon here and there,
Midnight moon everywhere,
Glowing in the winter sky,
Come with me and fly up high!

Georgia Kirkland & Bethany Roberts (9)
Aldbury Primary School

Viking Longship

Banded sails swinging in the stormy wind,
Attackers roaring and shouting,
Oars plunging into the spraying, stormy seas.

A golden dragon head on the horizon,
Lightning flashing out of thundery clouds,
The night darkening by the minute.

The Viking ship glancing through the slashing sea of the north,
The hard work of men jerking the ship,
Something's going to happen tonight.

Spencer Rance (8)
Aldwickbury School

I Like To Play Rugby

I like to play rugby, it's such fun,
But it would be even better if our team won!

While I'm playing the game,
I'm thinking of victorious fame,
Standing on the podium
And shouting out my name.

Michael Parsey (10)
Aldwickbury School

Voyage Of The Vikings

The Vikings set off as fast as a whale to reach the open sea,
Sharks attack but they are no match for the mighty Vikings.

They throw spears at the sharks and as fierce as they might seem,
The sharks have been defeated.
'Land ahoy!' shouts a warrior.

After battles at sea and attacks by sharks,
The Vikings have reached the Saxon village,
Breaking the waves as they hit the land.

Pouring out of their ship, the Vikings march to the village.
Grinding of metal is deafening.
They steal the Saxons' valuables
And head back to the ship.

Niles Webb (8)
Aldwickbury School

Long Ship Journey

Storming through the darkness
Smashing into waves
Sea spraying ferociously
Sail flapping frantically
Looks like we'll be out here for ages
It's so misty, we can't even see where we're rowing
The prow pushing the water aside
The golden head of the hound
Glistening in the moonlight.

Storming through the darkness
Flying through the water
The boat full of gold
The only thing on our minds is getting home.

Daniel Cobb (8)
Aldwickbury School

Viking Saga

I am a Viking,
Soaring through the stormy sea,
There goes the Golden Dragon,
Spray splashing in my face,
I'm as wet as the sea,
Seventy oars slashing through the salty sea,
The land disappears from sight,
The great eagle's wings flapping up and down,
The day suddenly turned into night,
The gale turned into a fearsome storm,
We carried on going through the night,
Only the moon to guide us,
Suddenly a mist arose,
It was as thick as a human body,
We couldn't even see ourselves,
Soon it disappeared and we saw land,
We could see ferocious rocks surrounding it,
Vikings could be seen attacking,
Britannia was fighting for all it was worth.
'Attack, attack!' shouted Britannia.
Forward went the ferocious Vikings
And we won the battle!

James Yurkwich (8)
Aldwickbury School

Bubble

B ubbles have circumference, you see it as they flow
U nderneath the bubbles is sun reflected glow
B ubbles have great colours
B ecause they shine like gold
L ots of bubbles popping when their life is done
E ven if it's windy, it's lots more fun!

Nico Bosatta (9)
Aldwickbury School

A Viking Poem

If I were a Viking
I would sail the seven seas
With a shimmering figurehead
Scaring all the surprised sailors

If I were a Viking
I would skid on the surface
Spraying the stormy weather
With a shower of the salty sea

If I were a Viking
I would make my men row
Like machines in birds' wings
Speeding through the seas

If I were a Viking
I would have strength like sumo wrestlers
Fighting my way through the Atlantic
To Greenland and beyond

But I'm not a Viking
So I can't sail the seven seas
And if I'm not soon asleep
Then trouble there will be.

Joseph Galliford (8)
Aldwickbury School

Bubbles

Bubbles, bubbles, glorious bubbles
They float, they duck, they glide
They are purple, gold, green and blue
They dance, they spin
They wriggle, they float
I love bubbles
Bubbles are great
They always make me laugh.

Sebastian Bretnall (9)
Aldwickbury School

My Magic Box

(Based on 'Magic Box' by Kit Wright)

I will put in the box . . .

Leaves suspended in the air
Sea rushing up the shore
The taste of chocolate

I will put in the box . . .

Pride and success
The bark of a dog
The joke of an old relative

I will put in the box . . .

Cures for illness
Happiness and joy
Love and care

My box is made from gold pearls
It has good deeds in the corners
Its hinges are made from mammoth tusks

I will ski in my box, down the hill
Landing on soft snow glowing white
From the sun.

Mark James (10)
Aldwickbury School

Bubbles

Bubbles, bubbles everywhere
Lots of different colours
Red, orange, blue and yellow
Green and many others
When blown by the wind they dance and sing
They duck and dive
They land
And . . .
Explode!

Christian Wilson (10)
Aldwickbury School

Magic Box

(Based on 'Magic Box' by Kit Wright)

I will put in my box . . .

The soul of a unicorn,
The breath of a lion panting on the hot plains of the savannah,
A sorcerer's pendant glistening red and green.

I will put in my box . . .

The treasure at the end of the rainbow,
A lucky, four-leafed clover,
The last snowflake that falls.

I will put in my box . . .

The smile of a baby,
The places I wish to go to,
A blue moon on a dark night.

I will put in my box . . .
The stars in the night sky,
The rustling of leaves on an autumn day,
The mind of an alien.

My box is fashioned with hinges made from lizard skin,
With the sky on the lid and stars in the corners.

I will swim in my box
Swim until the day is gone.

Jamie Brown (10)
Aldwickbury School

Bubbles

Bubbles, bubbles floating around
Bubbles, bubbles you are so big
Bubbles, bubbles you are so beautiful
Bubbles, bubbles floating around
Bubbles, bubbles, so many colours
Bubbles, bubbles you are colourful.

Edward Hales (9)
Aldwickbury School

The Magic Box

(Based on 'Magic Box' by Kit Wright)

I will put in my box . . .

The eye of a tornado
The first rainbow
And the last raindrop

I will put in my box . . .

The middle of the sun
The solar eclipse
And Saturn's ring

I will put in my box . . .

The second life
A cat's nine lives
And the first Christmas

My box is made of the armour of a Nazgûl
Carved by a mystical creature of the Ordan woods
And the hinges are made of serpent bones

In my box I shall race the penguins
On the great ice caps of Antarctica
And see all my memories on a giant TV.

Matthew Russell (10)
Aldwickbury School

Bubbles

I saw lots of bubbles one day
They made a nice array
They danced and dived and floated and twirled
That's the way bubbles move.
The colours they were pinks and purples
Greens and blues
Mauve and silver
Bubbles, they make me laugh
I like them when they dance.

Jack Forber (9)
Aldwickbury School

The Magic Box

(Based on 'Magic Box' by Kit Wright)

I will put in my box . . .

The single flame of a burning fire
A smell of a scented flower
A moon that's made of Camembert

I will put in my box . . .

The soft feather of a baby bird
The flutter by of a butterfly
The smell of bacon on a Sunday morning

I will put in my box . . .

The key to a secret garden
The rose of a hedgerow
And the chirp of a newborn chick

My box will be made from
Seagulls' feathers and flowers that never wilt,
The hinges will be made from rabbits' teeth
And a surprise in every corner.

I will dive into my box.

James Turner-Small (10)
Aldwickbury School

Bubbles

Bubbles fly and glide through the air
They are such fun to play with
Bubbles come in many colours
Red, blue, pink and green.
There is always more than one
When they start to pop
And are flying down to Earth
The fun ends.

Jack Leigh (9)
Aldwickbury School

My Magic Box

(Based on 'Magic Box' by Kit Wright)

I will put in my box . . .

A strange electric bird flying above the frozen sea
A chrome tiger sprinting through the jungle
It's another dimension to a different realm.

I will put in the box . . .

A massive rocket ship going to the moon
Stars twinkling in the sky
Another place above the universe, a different land.

I will put in the box . . .

A crouching tiger ready to strike its prey
A hidden dragon waiting to be discovered
A huge tidal wave ready to crash down.

My box is made of
Ice, fire, wind and earth
With silver hinges and
A golden lock.

Jordan Howell (10)
Aldwickbury School

Bubbles

Bubbles in the wind
Blue ones, purple ones
Green and orange.
All the different colours
Shivering, shooting
Blowing in the wind
Gliding, ducking, landing
Bursting, popping
Up and down and side to side
You can blow them
Do what you want really
They always dance in the air.

Sebastian Ferguson (9)
Aldwickbury School

Slava's Snow Show

S lava is a play
L ots of funny parts
A t Milton Keynes
V aried seat heights
A t the end huge balls and balloons come out
S o exciting

S lava is a play
N obody disliked it
O val was the theatre
W eird clowns were there

S lava is a play
H ow many people were there I don't know
O ther clowns played
W hen it was over I was so sad.

Sammee Bhatti (9)
Aldwickbury School

First Day

First day at school, I couldn't wait to go!
Had some new shoes that don't pinch my toe.
Lost my way to assembly, a kind prefect helped me out,
The spelling test was easy, not next time, I doubt.
The science got really messy, after the volcano erupted,
The Latin was fun with all the verbs we constructed.
Lunch was great, seconds in fish and chips,
Art was superb, we made a model of our hips.
Maths was the best because we started on angles,
Sport was fantastic, except the boots were all tangled.
In break I enjoyed the maths factory of pi,
In prep Tom's ink cartridge exploded over his tie.
At the end of the day I said goodbye to the boys,
And I sat down to mark, as they went home to their toys!

Charles Oliver (9)
Aldwickbury School

My Magic Box

(Based on 'Magic Box' by Kit Wright)

I will put in my box . . .

The key to Atlantis,
A dream I never dreamt,
A shooting star.

I will put in my box . . .

The darkest night,
A horn of a unicorn,
My first word.

I will put in my box . . .

An unpopulated world,
A baby's giggle,
My best memory.

My box will be fashioned with
Ruby for the lock and rose-gold for the corners,
The hinges are made from sabre-toothed tigers' teeth
And the frame made from platinum lined with tiger's eye.

I will create a new world in my box
With new animals and no illnesses,
New tastes and go to the future.

Mark Freeman (10)
Aldwickbury School

Bubbles

Bubbles, bubbles
Lovely bubbles
All different colours
Pink, blue
Red, gold and orange
Dance around
Go bubbles
Go free!

Michael Fielder (9)
Aldwickbury School

The Terror Torture

The ship coming, the waves breaking
The face is faking
We fled, death-defying
Skimming like a stone it comes.
It's coming gracefully,
Flying like a bird.

They're coming
They're coming
Run everyone
They're scanning every move.

Ten minutes till we're dead
Slashing swords sharing
Get our weapons, be brave.

They're coming
They're coming
Run everyone
They're scanning every move.

Five minutes now
Not long to go
Tired men, we're ready
Word of, 'High ho'.

They're coming
They're coming
Run everyone
They're scanning every move

Rory Armstrong (9)
Aldwickbury School

The Three Hags

The three hags were cackling
With long, matted hair
And long, claw-like fingers.
They had beady eyes and swayed like a wave
As they stepped.
Their bare, wrinkled feet stood
On the thistles on the heath.
They looked old and scary
They seemed chaotic
With high, shaky voices,
Faces covered with wrinkles.
Scared, dirty faces
Bad smells
Flying, hovering in the air
Mysterious
Skeletons beneath their thin flesh.

Toby Gatward (10)
Aldwickbury School

The Hag Sisters

Mwaa ha ha ha mwaa
We the hags, friend and foe
Upon this spiteful world
Purify the earth and stone
With bags of bones
We the sisters same to eye
Spy upon the stars
When we look
We see the future and the past
The rich, the poor, the damned
The hopeful
All command our will
But we are strong at heart.

Greg Conlin (10)
Aldwickbury School

I Will Put In My Box

I will put in my box . . .
A roaring wave
The smell of rich chocolate
The heat of fire

I will put in my box . . .
Loads of jelly
The sound of rain dropping
A huge chocolate factory
The Mediterranean

I will put in my box . . .
A house of chocolate that wouldn't melt
The smell of petrol
The snow brushing up when you're skiing

I will race with the planets
I will fill it with joy
I will surf the huge waves.

Michael Edwards (10)
Aldwickbury School

In My Dreams

In the day I think of things
I would like to happen in my dreams
But they do not come true
I dream of things that are really nice
But nothing I would like to do
I went to Hollywood
I was in my favourite TV show
But every night
When everything is going right
My dreams slip away into a lie.

Henry Webb (9)
Aldwickbury School

My Magic Box

(Based on 'Magic Box' by Kit Wright)

I will put in the box . . .

The cheer from a World Cup crowd,
The diamond key to Heaven,
The everlasting smile of my first puppy.

I will put in the box . . .

The first day of summer,
The swirl of the sea,
The taste of sweet chocolate.

I will put in the box . . .

The backbone of a lizard,
The memories of my past times,
The exit from Hell.

My box is comprised of gold and platinum,
With hinges of dinosaur bone.
The lid is structured from lizard muscle.

I shall swim in my box
In the deepest oceans and seas,
Then fly through the sky and back,
Just in time for tea.

Christopher Quelch (10)
Aldwickbury School

The Witches

In the gloomy, dark and scary heath
With howling winds
The eerie plains without sound
Bats fill the damp air

When trees sway with no leaves
You know evil is here
Beware of the heath, Macbeth
Here gather the weird sisters.

Joe Pearce (10)
Aldwickbury School

The Magic Box

(Based on 'Magic Box' by Kit Wright)

I will put in my box . . .

A place I never went to,
The laughter of a newborn baby,
The smell of newly mown grass.

I will put in my box . . .

A golden house gleaming in the sun,
A planet I never saw,
The smell of bacon on a Sunday morning.

I will put in my box . . .

The roar of a lion,
A fire on a winter night,
A soft feather of a bird.

My box is made of gold and wrapped in silk,
The hinges are made of the thorn of a blackberry bush.
I will fly into my box.
I will fly to South Africa and I will watch the animals.

Luke Dinwoodie (11)
Aldwickbury School

The Heath Of Scotland

One dark night, as the trees rustled and bustled
The witches stood with their open hoods
They said Macbeth would be king
But Banquo would follow
Only Banquo's son would get the hallows
Thunders crashed
Where everyone battled
The blood came out, there was no drought
Macbeth was killed, the people were thrilled.

Leo Barrett (10)
Aldwickbury School

The Magic Box

(Based on 'Magic Box' by Kit Wright)

I will put in the box . . .

My favourite dreams at night,
My favourite clothes,
My favourite football players.

I will put in the box . . .

My favourite books,
My favourite toys,
The fastest bowlers in the world.

I will put in the box . . .
My most happiest memories,
My most happiest moments on roller coasters,
My favourite birds of paradise.

I will put in the box . . .

My favourite noises,
My favourite cars,
My favourite colours.

I will put in the box . . .

The tip of a tongue touching wood,
The tip of a tongue touching steel,
The tip of a tongue touching glass.

My box is fashioned from gold, silver and violet,
With cold and warm blood on the lid,
My favourite football teams in the corners
And my favourite PS2 games make up the hinges.

I will play with my games consoles
And then I will travel far and wide to Hawaii.

Sarvesh Thiruchelvam (10)
Aldwickbury School

My Magic Box

(Based on 'Magic Box' by Kit Wright)

I will put in my box . . .

The battlefield of the 41st millennium
The sound of a gunshot
A treaty of peace.

I will put in my box . . .

The horn of a unicorn
The flickering eye of a dragon
A shining demon.

I will put in my box . . .

Mozart's first tune
The clash of a cymbal
The art of the drummer.

I will put in my box . . .

A fire on a winter's day
The ticking of an old clock
The first star.

My box is made from fire and ice
With rubies on the lid and gems in the corners
Its clasp is a clasp of darkness.

I will fight in my box
And save the galaxy
Then the gunfire will cease
And there will be peace at last.

Theo Dixon (10)
Aldwickbury School

The Magic Box

(Based on 'Magic Box' by Kit Wright)

I will put in the box . . .

An eye of a dragon,
An angel from Heaven
And the horns of the Devil.

I will put in the box . . .

A scale from a mermaid,
The rays of a blue sun
And the first hop of my rabbits.

I will put in the box . . .

The five pounds from my first tooth,
The ashes from the depths of Hell
And a wish from a wishing well.

I will put in the box . . .

A roar of a lion,
The venom of a cobra
And the blood from World War III.

My box is made with gold and silver,
With diamonds on the lid and emeralds in the corners.
The hinges are made from the claws of a phoenix.

I shall play football in my box
On the dark green grass of Wembley,
Then score the winning goal for Liverpool
With everybody cheering.

Arjun Patel (10)
Aldwickbury School

My Magic Box

(Based on 'Magic Box' by Kit Wright)

I will put in my box . . .

The staring gaze of a serpent's eye,
The solid tusk of a woolly mammoth,
The tip of a spear from a ruthless warrior.

I will put in my box . . .

Buried treasure from a long-lost pirate,
The taste of a chocolate egg at Easter,
A ray of sun which shines in the sky.

I will put in my box . . .

The rumble of an earthquake,
The calming rustle of the leaves,
The moaning whistle of the wind.

I will put in my box . . .

The sound of my first laugh,
The first mumble of a voice,
The cry of a baby.

My box is made from the oceans of the world
And the pyramids of Egypt,
With patterns of gold on the lid
And the animals of the world in the corners.
Its hinges are made from a dinosaur skeleton.

I will play sport in my box,
Scoring goals, hitting runs and smashing winners
In front of great roaring crowds,
The sun burning high.

George MacGregor (11)
Aldwickbury School

My Magic Box

(Based on 'Magic Box' by Kit Wright)

I will put in my box . . .

A cat with a bark and a dog with a purr,
A cuddle with my dogs,
The wing of a dragonfly and an eye of a hawk.

I will put in my box . . .

The glint of a third eye,
Wales winning the World Cup and
A snowman with a leek for a nose.

I will put in my box . . .

A diamond and an emerald,
The smell of a log fire and
Stag horns just coming through.

I will put in my box . . .

Pictures and memories,
A venomous snake and
My fabulous family.

My box is made from old oak wood.
My box's corners are made from gold and silver
And embroidered with rubies.
The hinges are made from a pensioner's old, creaky bones
And the lock is made from ancient gold.

I shall play in my box and
I shall look at the memories in my box.
I shall retreat to my box when I am upset.

Henry Woodthorpe (10)
Aldwickbury School

The Magic Box

(Based on 'Magic Box' by Kit Wright)

I will put in my box . . .

The breath of a fearless dragon
The horn of a great unicorn
The sword of the best ninja

I will put in my box . . .

The highest cloud in the sky
The light of the second sun
A ride on an elephant

I will put in my box . . .

The boots of Steven Gerrard
A cat's ninth life
The Pacific's water

I will put in my box . . .

The biggest fish ever
A butterfly's wing
The sun's blaze

My box is designed with dragon scales
With phoenix feathers on the lid and memories in the corners
Its hinges are made from dinosaur bones

I shall fly in my box
On a dragon so big and strong
Then ride on a unicorn
And get home for tea.

Alex Blakesley (10)
Aldwickbury School

My Magic Box

(Based on 'Magic Box' by Kit Wright)

I'll put in my box . . .

The dream of winning Wimbledon,
The eyes of a dragon,
My first word 'dirty'.

I'll put in my box . . .

The dream of setting a record,
The dream of flying high in the sky,
The dream of being famous.

I'll put in my box . . .

The memories of my first tennis match,
When I first went to school,
Seeing me in my own team colours.

I'll put in my box . . .

The dream of climbing the tallest mountain,
To swim to the bottom of the sea,
To be the first man on the sun.

It's made from fine tiger skin,
A hint of diamond and sapphire jewels,
In the corners it has got wings to fly.

In my box there are no rules,
Rollerskate to the top of the mountain,
You can be transformed,
But there's no escape.

James Wilkinson (11)
Aldwickbury School

The Magic Box

(Based on 'Magic Box' by Kit Wright)

I will put in the box . . .

The first glimpse of Mount Everest,
The first boat on the River Nile,
The first person on Earth.

I will put in the box . . .

The smell of a sweet strawberry,
The taste of warm chocolate,
The sound of crunching carrots.

I will put in the box . . .

When trees start to move,
When dinosaurs come back to life,
When zombies invaded Earth.

I will put in the box . . .

My first goal for Wheathampstead,
Harpenden winning the county cup,
Getting 36 not out for Aldwickbury School.

I will put in the box . . .

England winning the 1966 World Cup,
Man United becoming a team
And when the world comes to an end.

My box is made with
The first carved wood,
With diamonds on the lid and eyes in the corner,
The hinges are the creak of my bridge.

I shall score the winning goal in my box
For Manchester United,
Scoring to win the first ever quadruple.

Joey Jackson (11)
Aldwickbury School

The Magic Box

(Based on 'Magic Box' by Kit Wright)

I will put in my box . . .

A serpent's tooth
A lost budgie
The rubble of four towers

I will put in my box . . .

A group of little goblins
A pointing hand to lead my way
A house of a thousand rooms

I will put in my box . . .

A pond that leads to a black hole
A memory from eighteen birds
The stab of the first knife

I will put in my box . . .

An elephant's trunk
A wall of bananas and oranges
A group of black knights to guard me

My box will be fashioned from
Skulls of all sizes
Trees made from lava in the corners
Its hinges are the teeth of tigers
Its feet are bears' legs
A cobra's skeleton for the clasp
Rhino horns surround my box

I shall live in a small camp made with tents
Fly to a thousand islands
Look after countless livestock
Eat fish of all types.

Benjamin Hall (10)
Aldwickbury School

The Magic Box

(Based on 'Magic Box' by Kit Wright)

I will put in my box . . .

The first snowflake of winter,
The first leaf to fall in autumn
And the first flower of spring.

I will put in my box . . .

The memory of going to Wembley,
The memory of going to Lord's
And the memory of going to Twickenham.

I will put in my box . . .

A dragon's nostril,
A phoenix's feather
And the horn of a unicorn.

I will put in my box . . .

An eighth day of the week,
A 32nd day of the month
And a 367th day of the year.

My box is fashioned from snow,
With wishes in the corners,
Hinges made from ice.

I shall swim in my box,
Across the windy Atlantic
And wash ashore in Jamaica.

William Butterworth (10)
Aldwickbury School

The Magic Box

(Based on 'Magic Box' by Kit Wright)

I will put in my box . . .

The click of a grandfather clock
The sound of my pen on paper
The sound of the wind blowing on harp strings

I will put in my box . . .

The golden egg from a very small hen
A cat's ninth life
The longest flame of the sun

I will put in my box . . .

A piece of straw from the first thatched roof
Thc lowest cloud in the sky
My favourite colour, blue

I will put in my box . . .

The first potter's hand
The day I got my Liverpool kit
My goal that got us into the final

The lid of my box is made of the finest leather
The clasp is made of a dragon's head
The corners are special things

In my box I will jump off a cliff
And land on a phoenix's back
Its tail is a very hot blazing fire.

Tom Galliford (11)
Aldwickbury School

My Magic Box

(Based on 'Magic Box' by Kit Wright)

I will put in my box . . .

A swirling vortex,
The first light of the sun,
A snake's forked tongue.

I will put in my box . . .

A cloud's silver lining,
The first drop of a waterfall,
A spider's web glistening with dew on a sunny day.

I will put in my box . . .

The first word of a parrot,
Aladdin's magic carpet,
Merlin's hat.

I will put in my box . . .

My first birthday,
The feeling of hitting a six at Lord's
The goal that would win the World Cup for England.

My box will be made out of . . .

The finest oak with diamonds encrusted on it.
It shall be wrapped in the finest silk
With dreams in the corners.
Its lock will be made out of dragon bone
And the key made out of gold from the deepest mine.

I will dive into my box and swim in the deepest oceans
And land on a beach,
Where I will drive across the desert in a Jeep
And arrive to see England beat Australia
To win the cricket World Cup.

Milo Knights (10)
Aldwickbury School

The Magic Box

(Based on 'Magic Box' by Kit Wright)

I will put in my box . . .

The ashes of a Chinese dragon
The relief that my operation was over
The first sparkle of a newborn fairy

I will put in my box . . .

The first golden leaf that falls to the ground
A drip of blood from Dracula's tooth
A phoenix feather the colour of fire

I will put in my box . . .

The bark of Molly the dog when she first came in
The ears of Mickey Mouse
My mum's fantastic cooking

I will put in my box . . .

A baby's tooth
The first word out of the dictionary
My first word to the world

My box is fashioned by the most beautiful sunset
With rhino horns for hinges
And words of wisdom in the corners.
It has the smell of chocolate
And rubies on the lid.

I shall swim in my box
With the deep Atlantic Ocean fish with shiny scales,
Then get on a boat and drink out of coconuts
Filled with apple juice.

Christian Boothby (10)
Aldwickbury School

The Magic Box

(Based on 'Magic Box' by Kit Wright)

I will put in the box . . .

The cheer of fans when their team has just scored,
The fright of a thunderstorm,
The cry of a blue tit.

I will put in the box . . .

The taste of an Atlantic swordfish,
The bark of the first oak tree,
The feeling of triumph after victory.

I will put in the box . . .

Gandalf the White's ancient staff,
A witch cackling away at midnight,
William Shakespeare's last ever play.

I will put in the box . . .

A baby's first noise,
The answers to the universe
And the fire of an ancient volcano.

My box is fashioned from rubies and emeralds,
With memories of childhood in every corner.
Its clasp is from the prison, Alcatraz.

I travel in my box,
To every country on Earth
And take a picture of every country
For an album that I shall keep forever.

Ben Dubowitz (11)
Aldwickbury School

The Magic Box

(Based on 'Magic Box' by Kit Wright)

I will put in my box . . .

The Beano which I buy every week,
My family which I love so much,
A piano so I can play every day.

I will put in my box . . .

The memory of my first football match at West Ham,
My teddy, which I lost on a plane,
The dream of playing at Wembley.

I will put in my box . . .

The horn of a rhino on top of Mount Everest,
A mountain of chocolate and sweets,
A green moon, a trillion miles from Earth.

My box is made from all colours of the rainbow
And diamond encrusted platinum.
My hinges will be gold,
Made by the dwarves in the east.

I shall be king in my box
And govern all lands, near and far
And all points of the compass.
I will be king for a billion years,
Then fall into the deepest of sleeps,
Dreaming till the world breaks into a million pieces.

Max Cadman (10)
Aldwickbury School

My Magic Box

(Based on 'Magic Box' by Kit Wright)

I will put in my box . . .

The first picture of Bigfoot,
The giggle of a baby,
The last flame of a volcano.

I will put in my box . . .

The first step on Mars,
The growl of a tiger circling its prey,
The purr of a kitten.

I will put in my box . . .

A purple moon that orbits my house,
A room filled with rubies,
The twinkle of a glass eye.

I will put in my box . . .

Three wishes of Aladdin,
The first conversation with aliens,
A cat with 18 lives.

My box is fashioned with . . .

Dinosaur bones for the lid,
Lions' teeth for hinges
And alpine rock for the rest.

Luke Dawson (10)
Aldwickbury School

Autumn

A ll the time autumn is mystery
U mbrellas breaking here and there
T rick or treating is so much fun
U nder the tree where the children play
M onsters growling, roaring and moaning
N othing's better than October's spooky nights.

Cai Antoine (8)
Chorleywood Primary School

Autumn Poem

A corns falling on the ground with reflected sunshine
U mbrellas falling on the heads of the undead
T rick or treating is such fun
U nder the graves of the undead lives the greatest ghost
M onsters thinking they are human
N ovember, November, sunlight under the breeze of the undead.

Liam Rogers (8)
Chorleywood Primary School

Autumn

A corns fall on the ground, squirrels eat them
U mbrellas are everywhere every day
T rick or treating is so much fun
U nder my bed it is cold and cobwebby
M um cleans all of the cobwebs
N ovember, it's Hallowe'en, hooray!

Elise Bugeja (7)
Chorleywood Primary School

Autumn

A nimals hibernate here and there
U mbrellas break inside out
T rick or treating naughty children
U nder the ground the dead gather
M onster masks round every corner
N ovember nights are really scary.

Matthew Leveridge (8)
Chorleywood Primary School

Autumn

A utumn days and naughty nights
U sing conkers to have conker fights
T ake a look outside at night
U nlike normal nights
M oany ghosts are out
N ow you know what it is like on an autumn night.

David Edrop (8)
Chorleywood Primary School

Autumn

A corns and leaves falling off the trees
U mbrellas up in the rain
T rick or treating in the night
U ndo your costume ready for bed
M onsters crawling outside
N ight-time fireworks flash.

Phoebe Bird (7)
Chorleywood Primary School

Autumn

A utumn acorns everywhere
U ndead coming, better be scared
T rick or treaters collecting sweets
U mbrellas up
M onsters coming
N ervous children in the night.

Yusuf Ali (7)
Chorleywood Primary School

Clouds

Wispy and white up in the sky
Sleeping and snoring there they lie
From morning to eve they sit and they wait
In summer and autumn they stay up late
But in winter and spring they're such a trouble
Shouting and crying till it feels there are double
But when the gold sun begins to sink
They turn yellow, orange and bright pink
Hanging there they are the same
Just waiting and waiting is their aim.

Ema Nightingale (10)
Chorleywood Primary School

Autumn

A corns fall from trees
U nder my bed is my costume
T rick or treaters are at the door
U mbrellas are everywhere
M asks on children's faces
N ervous October nights.

Faith Ratcliff (7)
Chorleywood Primary School

Sea

The sea dancing joyfully in the moonlight
Swaying in the wind so silently.
The moonlight shining on the clapping sea
That's splashing happily against the shore.
Then the sea starts waving tiredly
Until there is not a stir and the sea falls asleep.

Ewan Cockburn (10)
Chorleywood Primary School

Sea

The sea and the waves are playing happily,
Clapping their hands together,
Deafeningly.
Suddenly, the sea shouts angrily,
As the storm sets in,
For now they are arguing noisily.

Calmer, calmer,
As the storm goes away.
Calmer, calmer,
Calm.

Lucy Addicott (10)
Chorleywood Primary School

Sea

The sea playing creatively
And spinning cautiously.
Bashing angrily,
Crying soundlessly,
Clapping joyfully
And bundling playfully.

Sean Cleveland (10)
Chorleywood Primary School

The Sea

Resting sleepily in the dark of night,
Whistling quietly like a bird,
The sea waving happily at the shore,
Dancing in the moonlight
And running over the sand.

Louis Dromard (10)
Chorleywood Primary School

Flames

The flames dance playfully,
An ever-changing beast.
Joyfully leaping into the cold night,
Chasing the stars.
Constantly licking at the wood,
Happily playing with themselves,
Hungrily devouring all in their path,
Until they die away,
The embers smoking silently.

Megan Stephens (10)
Chorleywood Primary School

Flames

As the flames start roaring
And the wind starts whistling
Through the trees.
As the flames start dancing
And flicking to and fro.
Feeding, it gets bigger,
Hissing like an angry snake,
Spitting out the embers
At passing people.

Samuel Topping (10)
Chorleywood Primary School

Flames

Flames devour the forest greedily
Dancing over the trees in their game of destruction
The flames beckon the rain to challenge them
Walking forward, setting fire to the grass
Striding towards the village.

Alex Morrison (10)
Chorleywood Primary School

Flames

Flames demolish the woods,
Dancing skilfully through the trees, waving furiously,
Destroying everything in their path,
Eating the wood loudly without hesitation,
Swaying dangerously in the wind,
Spitting rudely at trees,
Playing unfairly with the environment,
Hissing vengefully at things.

Joshua Putta (10)
Chorleywood Primary School

Cloud

The cloud slept silently
Waiting for the sun to come out.
The cloud smiled happily at the sunrise
But then it saw the grey sky.
So the cloud sadly cried.
The children came outside
The cloud waved merrily,
Gently whispered the cloud.

Amber Dyer (10)
Chorleywood Primary School

Cloud

The cloud smiled joyfully
At the oak tree,
Dancing happily in the sun.
The clouds slept silently
Under the warm moon,
But woke crying in the night.

George Goad (10)
Chorleywood Primary School

Moon

The moon, gazing sleepily
At the people strolling by.
Dancing gracefully,
Glides the silent moon.
Playing joyfully
With the planets.
Whispering silently
To the trees down below.
Glowing happily to the world
Below her.
Lovely shimmering moon.

Lili Baron (10)
Chorleywood Primary School

Snow

Dancing snow
Drifting across with the wind
Happily playing with other snowflakes
As they fall down
Staring at the cold ground
As they land
Calmly starting to fall asleep.

Diana Powell (10)
Chorleywood Primary School

Flames

On the bonfire the flames are dancing,
On the wood they're gracefully prancing,
Crackling and spitting, leaping high,
But when the night is done,
The flames will die.

Erica Jackson (10)
Chorleywood Primary School

The Clock

Not a sound escapes,
As the clock in the hall awakes,
Unblinkingly staring at the eternal blackness,
Slowly swaying this way and that,
Its pendulum of gold catches the only light.
As light starts to appear,
It starts to whistle merrily with the birds,
As it hears the yawning lord,
It becomes . . . silent.

George Nixon (10)
Chorleywood Primary School

Moon

The moon, dancing bouncily,
Peers secretly into houses of people.
To Mars shyly whispers the moon,
Playing joyfully with the stars.
His skipping cheerfully slows down
To a sleepy stroll,
Then to sleeping silently,
Sssshhh.

Chantelle Davies (10)
Chorleywood Primary School

Pianos

The piano was gently playing
Dancing gracefully
Beautifully it was singing
Suddenly sleeping
Peacefully.

Oliver Burks (11)
Chorleywood Primary School

Moon

The moon swiftly dancing
Smiling happily all night
The cheekily winking moon
Walking smoothly in the dark
While waving wistfully
She is swaying silently
Listening quietly with the stars
Until she falls asleep
Sleeping deeply all day long
Snoring loudly until
She wakes the next night.

Emma Cochrane (10)
Chorleywood Primary School

Piano

The piano is singing loudly
As it is jumping madly
Stamping angrily
But all of a sudden
It is sleeping
Peacefully.

Jack Deanus (10)
Chorleywood Primary School

Kettle

The kettle was thirsty for a drink
It was gradually shaking, playing madly
The bubbles inside blowing constantly
All of a sudden whistling loudly
Calming down peacefully.

Liam Keane (10)
Chorleywood Primary School

Henry VIII

Hampton Court as big as a war zone
Clothes like the finest silk
Jewellery as shiny as twinkling stars
Doorknobs as shiny as crystal stones
Trumpets as loud as fireworks in the shimmering sky
People as rich as a king or queen
Food that smells like a Christmas dinner
Henry VIII's belly as bulgy as ten watermelons.

Chloe Travers (8)
Chorleywood Primary School

Autumn

A nimals hibernating everywhere
U mbrellas are up all over the street
T rick or treating through the night
U mbrellas all over the floor
M umbling monsters through the night
N ovember spooky nights.

Lauren Beattie (7)
Chorleywood Primary School

Autumn

A corns falling off the trees
U mbrellas up in the sun
T rick or treating in the night
U ndo your warm boots ready to go
M onsters outside your house
N ight-time rockets crash.

Abigail Taylor (8)
Chorleywood Primary School

Untitled

The floor is as shiny as golden emeralds.
Kings as rich as Gordon Brown, Tony Blair
And Queen Elizabeth II.
Servants as brilliant as one hundred kings.
Jewellery like sparkly pools.

Jake Sejpal (8)
Chorleywood Primary School

Tudor Poem

Feast as big as Henry VIII
Hampton Court Palace as big as Wembley Stadium
Duck as big as the world
School felt as big as Henry's bedroom.

Sophie Ensor (8)
Chorleywood Primary School

Tudor Poem

Ceilings as beautiful as Heaven
Henry VIII as fat as a pig
Jewellery as shiny as shooting stars.

Jay Bugeja (8)
Chorleywood Primary School

Tudor Feasts

Food like the finest wine,
Clothes like glittering stars,
Curtains with the finest patterns,
Like a beautiful china vase.

Rosalie Davies (8)
Chorleywood Primary School

Tudor Times

Hampton Court as big as London
Clothes as warm as the sun
Bedding like big, puffy sheep
People as giant as a peach
A feast as big as twenty massive war fields
Plates as big and huge as a hundred spectacular fields.

Amy Patel (8)
Chorleywood Primary School

Terrible Tudors

Clothes comfortable as cushions
Doors like silver
Food as tasty as ice cream
Beds that smell like lavender.

Zoë Putta (8)
Chorleywood Primary School

Tudor Feasts

King Henry VIII as rich as a diamond
Hampton Court as tall as the Empire State Building
Doors as big as houses
The feasts were as big as an elephant.

Christian Toouli (9)
Chorleywood Primary School

Hampton Court

Hampton Court as big as a war zone,
Inside it's like a miniature Heaven,
The food in there as expensive as gold,
It is as big as 50 estates!

Sam Lee (8)
Chorleywood Primary School

Baby At School

One day a little baby had the urge to go to school.
The teachers got frustrated because all it did was drool.
The teachers had a meeting and decided it was cruel,
They said, 'We can't blame the baby, even if it only drools.'
Miss Tiny went to Mothercare to buy a little cot,
But it was no good when she realised it was the food she had forgot.
Mr Mackerel went again but tinned milk was all he got,
They left the cot in the fridge and it began to rot.
The teachers sighed, 'Babies are hard work!'

Hannah Lee (9)
Chorleywood Primary School

The Tudors

Clothes made of the finest silk
Carpets as soft as the feathers of a bird
Ponds as deep as a vast ocean
Diamonds as shiny as the reflecting moon
Food as tasty as sugary sweets
Curtains with patterns like bark on the trees
Jewels as beautiful as silver
Fires as hot as a volcano's lava.

Hamilton Campbell-Stanway (8)
Chorleywood Primary School

Tudor Feasts

Dining rooms as big as restaurants
Feasts like 24 Christmas dinners
Turkeys as big as the world
Tables as big as Wembley Stadium.

Anna Beaman (8)
Chorleywood Primary School

Rabbits And Ostriches

Rabbits:
They are cute
They are fluffy
They have long ears
They have big feet
They have a lucky rabbit's foot

Ostriches:
They have feathers
They have a long neck
They have big feet
They have a brain smaller than the eye
An ostrich can't fly.

Robert Everett (9)
Chorleywood Primary School

Tudor Times

A doorknob as golden as a gold crystal,
Clothes as soft as pillows,
A feast as big as a football pitch,
Jewellery like glittering flames,
Jewellery as silver as stars,
The ceiling as bright as twinkling, shiny stars.

Jasmine Attwood (8)
Chorleywood Primary School

Tudor Poem

Clothes as soft as velvet
Kings as rich as they can get
Flags as red as a burning fire
King Henry as fat as a pig.

Owen Blackwell (8)
Chorleywood Primary School

Books

When you open a book
You'll soon find out
That it can take you all about!

Into a world
Only you can see
Come and join the fun with me!

Someone calls 'dinner'
You don't hear your mum
You're in a bookie world of fun!

Come into my world
Fun you'll find
Your mother definitely won't mind!

I'll have to go now
Your imagination's falling
And I'm sure I hear your mother calling!
Goodbye!

Victoria Leeman (10)
Chorleywood Primary School

The Mysterious Cloakroom

When you enter the mysterious cloakroom,
You'll soon find out what I'm going on about!
If you hang your coat up for the rest of the night,
You'll soon find out, you'll have to fight!
When you come back in the morning,
Your coat will be gone.
When your nan picks you up,
You'll be old with cold!

Madeleine Jones (9)
Chorleywood Primary School

Shopping

S ales, I love them
H andbags, leather and velvet
O range earrings gleaming
P rimark is . . .
P erfect
I ndigo V-necks models wear
N ecklaces blue and purple
G ot to have lots of belts.
Awesome!

Isabella Hyde (9)
Chorleywood Primary School

Benjamin

B rilliant at talking to himself
E verything in the world he did not make
N ever thinks he has done his work
J unior Ben is in Year 5
A lways doubts himself
M arvellous Ben likes football
I like cake
N ow I must go.

Ben Jessett (9)
Chorleywood Primary School

Me

L ovely
I ntelligent
B right
B eautiful
Y oung.

Liberty Pickett (9)
Chorleywood Primary School

Alex Trevett

A lex wishes to run the
L ondon marathon
E ven he is very fast and for
X mas he wants a sports car

T oast he will eat for breakfast, he will
R oar at the lions and
E at his enemies, also
V anquish the villains
E xecute murderers
T ame the beast
T ame Alex.

Alex Trevett (9)
Chorleywood Primary School

Me

R eally great
O verly cool
S tylish
I diotic
E xtraordinary

O dd
L oud
E xcited
A rgues a lot
R ules
Y ay for me!

Rosie O'Leary (9)
Chorleywood Primary School

Autumn Days

Autumn days the sky is steel
And the magpie began to steal.
Shiny brown conkers that are wrapped in spikes
And a silky coat inside,
The children play in the autumn leaves and the large conker tree.
Smell of pine needles and of the fresh, new autumn air.
A nice warm house to play in when it gets cold.
To cook a fresh dinner with a hot stove and a warm bed in the night.
Wind whistling through the chimney pots, but we are warm inside.
While it is cold outdoors, the dawn struck with a freezing wind
And the clocks turning back to one hour before,
But school is shut for cable repairs.
Birds migrate by flying south and the bear begins to hibernate.
A thorny bush is covered in blackberries
And is being picked right now while people prepare for Christmas.
Buying presents and decorations while autumn is ignored,
But its beauty remains through the whole season.
But never does it change, leaves of orange, red and green
Fall upon the ground like confetti in front of a bride and groom.
An apple pie is made of warm apple sauce
And a large roast dinner is made.
Fireworks crackle and bonfires flare and crackle.
Children begin to sing, remember the 5th of November
And adults tend the flame.
A black cloud like a jet floats in the air,
Sending rain down like a floating, ever-full, upside-down bucket.
Flowers wither and shed their seeds as the cold envelops them.
The trees provide shelter for nests and a safe home for animals.
Then winter comes.

Rennan Tilbury (8)
Hartsfield JMI School

Kangaroo Began

(Based on 'Cat Began' by Andrew Matthews)

Kangaroo began:
She took the inside of the handbag
She took the brownness of a toffee
And made her pouch.

For her coat:
She took the brownness of a well-watered tree
She took the smoothness of a baby's bottom.

For her bounce:
She took the up and down of a pogo stick
She took the fur of a big trampoline.

For her bottom:
She took the smell of a baby's bottom
She took the sweatiness of a foot.

For her ears:
She took the point of a pin
She took the cuteness of a newborn baby
And Kangaroo was made.

Megan Pain (9)
Hartsfield JMI School

Autumn Ways

In autumn I can see all the trees swaying side to side,
As if they are dancing with each other.
I can see all the different people with their umbrellas,
As it is getting much wetter.
I can hear all of the coloured leaves falling on the ground,
Getting trampled on and crunching.
I can hear all the wind making a growling noise
As it runs down the street.
I can smell all the gases from the cars
As nobody is walking because it's too wet.

Megan Neale (9)
Hartsfield JMI School

Dog Began

(Based on 'Cat Began' by Andrew Matthews)

Dog began:
He took the growling from the lion
He took the howling from the wolf
And made his voice.

For his coat:
He took the roughness from sandpaper
He took the hardness from the cupboard door.

For his eyes:
He took the twinkle from the star
He took the yellow from the sun.

For his colour:
He took the black from the bat
He took white from the summer cloud.

For his teeth:
He took the sharpness from the shark
He took the white from the white chocolate
And Dog was made.

Amy Le Sage (9)
Hartsfield JMI School

Autumn Poem

Pumpkins in windows, people knocking on doors
Leaves crunching on the floor as you walk by
Smoke crowding out of chimneys warming thousands of houses
Fireworks shooting in the air and erupting, *bang, bang, bang!*
Dramatic diamond rockets flying in the air.

Alex Wright (8)
Hartsfield JMI School

Gorilla Began

(Based on 'Cat Began' by Andrew Matthews)

Gorilla began:
He took the hair of the bear
He took the toes of the human
He took the feet of the tiger
And made his legs.

For his coat:
He took the roughness of a woolly jumper
He took the black of space.

For his ears:
He took the ears of a human
He took the ear holes of the cheetah.

For his eyes:
He took the colour of a plant
He took the eyebrows of a lady.

For his mouth:
He took the lips of a cheetah
He took the teeth of a lion
And Gorilla was made.

Robert Coldrey (9)
Hartsfield JMI School

Autumn Fun

A utumn leaves spiralling down
U mbrellas flapping in the wind
T he times are changing
U nusual things are happening
M ajestic rockets rising
N ever been more fun than autumn.

Adam Orton (8)
Hartsfield JMI School

An Autumn Poem

Children dressed in costumes for Hallowe'en
Pumpkins with candles in
Fireworks going off
The crack of conkers, so much to find.

Ruby-red rockets rising
Green apples, so nice to eat
Apple pie I can taste
Children knocking on doors. *Bang, bang, bang!*

Bare trees with no leaves
Children shouting, 'Trick or treat?'
Smoke from the bonfire
Candy cracking, conkers clapping
Toffee apples, nice and sticky
Autumn apples, amazing autumn.

Bethany Harley (8)
Hartsfield JMI School

Autumn Days

I can see leaves falling and blowing about
Leaves dancing around and around
Shiny conkers falling from the trees
Fireworks getting ready to go

Birds singing and flying south
People stepping on crunchy leaves
Brown leaves like chocolate
Feeling shiny conkers
Amazing autumn is amazing
I can smell bonfire smoke
Tasting the wind is fantastic
I can hear the wind blowing
Leaves flying, coming in the classroom.

Neil Angus
Hartsfield JMI School

What Happens In Autumn

In autumn I can see red, orange and yellow leaves
Falling from the trees.
I can see fields icy as a skating rink.
I can hear birds flying south.
The leaves rustling, dancing about
And the strong wind rustling in my ears.
I can smell bonfires.
Smoke coming out of the chimney pots
And the wet bark everywhere.
My hot cocoa in my flask
And my delightful chocolate bar.
I can touch coldness
And the old leaves on the ground.
Squirrels scuttling along the path
And that's my autumn poem.

Kiara Cesvette (9)
Hartsfield JMI School

Autumn

Autumn is a wonderful season.
It is a time of year when leaves fall down
And the leaves turn brown and yellow.

I can hear the leaves crunching
And hear people sneezing for winter.

I can smell bonfires
And I can smell the fresh air.

I can taste hot chocolate
And roast dinner.

I can touch frosted leaves
And I can touch frosted branches as well.

Some of the leaves are as red as the sun,
Other leaves are as brown as a chair.

Roshan Panarkar
Hartsfield JMI School

Meerkat

(Based on 'Cat Began' by Andrew Matthews)

Meerkat began
He took the squeak of a mouse
He took the rustle of the leaves
And made his voice

For his coat
He took the furry grass
He took the goldness of a penny

For his walk
He took the speed of an Olympic racer
He took the walk of an Egyptian king

For his eyes
He took the shine of the sun
He took the sparkle of the stars

For his size
He took the size of a newborn baby
He took the roots of the biggest tree
And Meerkat was made.

Adam Dixon (9)
Hartsfield JMI School

Autumn Is The Best

Suddenly autumn has come!
The days are coming in colder,
The trees are going side to side softly.

Then you see sparkling fireworks in the air.
Bang!
Leaves falling and turning brown, yellow, red
And falling off the trees.

I can feel the really cold air
And the fireworks as hot as fire.

Nathan Allen (8)
Hartsfield JMI School

Autumn Is Coming

Autumn is coming soon . . .

I'm ready for the rustling leaves crunching in my ear.
Soon there will be breezy brown leaves going up and down
in my head.

Then I will be able to see the frosty fields
And also the bushes going *swish, swash* every second.

Then autumn came . . .

Now I can hear the rustling leaves like they're crunching in my ear.
Now I can see the breezy brown leaves going up and down
in my head.

And now I can see the frosty fields
And all the time I can see the bushes going *swish, swash*
every second.

The winter came . . .

Lucy Brewer (8)
Hartsfield JMI School

In Autumn

In autumn I can see my breath because it's so cold
Brown leaves fall off the trees gently
I can see a sky full of clouds.

There is a sea of leaves crunching
I can hear the wind blowing hard
There are birds tweeting as they fly south
It is as cold as ice.

The leathery leap in the wind
I will soon smell bonfires on Bonfire Night.
I'm tasting air as I breathe
I can touch brown leaves.
In autumn I step on leaves and they crunch.

Max Piner (8)
Hartsfield JMI School

Horse Began

(Based on 'Cat Began' by Andrew Matthews)

Horse began:
She took the rushing of the river
She took the rumble of an earthquake
And made her voice.

For her coat:
She took the softness of velvet
She took the thickness of leather.

For her walk:
She took the speed of lightning
She took the sound of the howling wind.

For her eyes:
She took the shine of a mirror
She took the shape of the full moon.

For her temperament:
She took the calmness of the breeze
She took the courage of the lion's heart
And Horse was made.

Milly Green (10)
Hartsfield JMI School

Autumn Poem

Pumpkin pie, toast and candy,
That's what I can taste,
Leaves crunching and bare trees,
Conkers cracking too.
Listen for the trick or treat
As children ask for candy.
It's candy cracking, conkers clapping.
Autumn apples, amazingly awesome.
I can smell the hog roast and fresh conkers too,
Autumn is the crunch of apple pie.

Albert Taylor (9)
Hartsfield JMI School

Puppy Began

(Based on 'Cat Began' by Andrew Matthews)

Puppy began:
She took the wailing of the white wolf
She took the sweetness of strawberries and cream
And made her voice

For her coat:
She took the comfort of the cushion
She took the shimmer of the sun

For her walk:
She took the slowness of a snail
She took the silence of the night

For her eyes:
She took the sparkle of an earring
She took the brightness of the moon

For her teeth:
She took the sharpness of a tiger's canine
She took the whiteness of a piece of paper
And Puppy was made.

Alexandra Mitchell (9)
Hartsfield JMI School

Autumn Days

Leaves crunching on the ground
Hats to keep your head warm
Firework signs up in shops
Conkers banging on my head as if they want to come in
I can hear leaves rustling in the trees
Sticks cracking on the ground as you tread on them
Conkers lying on the ground like feathers.

Amelia Cummins
Hartsfield JMI School

Tiger Began

(Based on 'Cat Began' by Andrew Matthews)

Tiger began:
She took the roar of the sea
She took the wail of the wind
And made her voice

For her coat:
She took the shimmer of the stars
She took the softness of a feather

For her walk:
She took the pride of a winner
She took the pounce of a cat

For her eyes:
She took the glimpse of the moon
She took the sharpness of a needle

For her markings:
She took the blinding orange of the sun
She took the stripes of the dark night sky
And Tiger was made.

Ruby Chalkley (10)
Hartsfield JMI School

My Autumn Poem

A re you ready for another autumn?
U nusual things are happening
T he trees' leaves are turning beautiful red, brown and orange
U mbrellas are popping up ready for the rain
M y wellies are sliding onto my feet ready for splashing in puddles
N ow it's time for sleep.

Jamie Allen (9)
Hartsfield JMI School

Dog Began

(Based on 'Cat Began' by Andrew Matthews)

Dog began:
He took the howl of the tornado
He took the rush of the water
And made his voice.

For his coat:
He took the colours of autumn
He took the sparkle of ice

For his walk:
He took the crackle of the fire
He took the speed of a cheetah

For his eyes:
He took the sparkle of a diamond
He took the black of the night

For his teeth:
He took the point of the pencil
He took the gleam of the stars
And Dog was made.

George Muge (9)
Hartsfield JMI School

Autumn

A re you ready for another autumn?
U mbrellas going inside out from the blustery wind
T angy mince pies for the midnight snack are tasty indeed
U ncooked chicken ready to be roasted
M y family come to enjoy autumn with me
N ow night has fallen the fun is over and we can get ready for
another day.

Christopher Hayes (8)
Hartsfield JMI School

Tiger Began

(Based on 'Cat Began' by Andrew Matthews)

Tiger began:
He took the roar of an engine
He took the beat of a drum
And made his voice.

For his coat:
He took the softness of a pillow
He took the marks of his breed

For his walk:
He took the stride of a king
He took the style of a supermodel

For his eyes:
He took the blackness of the night sky
He took the roundness of a coin

For his teeth:
He took the sharpness of an icicle
He took the toughness of a rock
And Tiger was made.

Alex Bowles
Hartsfield JMI School

Autumn Time Is Here

Autumn time has started
Rain is falling down
There are leaves falling off the trees
Then dancing on the ground
Conkers falling on the ground
As children start collecting
I can hear rain going *pitter-patter, pitter-patter* on the windows
It's hard to get to sleep.

Abigail Foggo (8)
Hartsfield JMI School

Cat Began

(Based on 'Cat Began' by Andrew Matthews)

Cat began:
He took the whistling of the wind
He took the purr of the car engine

For his coat:
He took the light brown of a tree trunk
He took the blades of grass

For his walk:
He took the pitter-patter of the rain
He took the silence of the mouse

For his eyes:
He took the sparkle of the stars
He took the dark green of the grass

For his fur:
He took the dark brown of chocolate
He took the light of day
And Cat was made.

Joe Penny (10)
Hartsfield JMI School

Autumn

The wind in the trees,
Leaves dancing in the gusts.
Kids jumping in puddles.
Leaves as brown as chocolate,
Frost freezing fingertips.

Cars splashing by,
People soaking wet.
I'm stuck indoors,
Crawling on the floor.

Thomas Baxter (8)
Hartsfield JMI School

Scorpion Began

(Based on 'Cat Began' by Andrew Matthews)

Scorpion began:

He took the pierce of a needle
He took the prick of an earring
And made his sting

For his shell:

He took the protectiveness of an iron shield
He took the strength of a knight

For his walk:
He took the scuttle of a crab
He took the speed of an F1 racing car

For his eyes:

He took the colour of a carrot
He took the darkness of a pitch-black sky

For his agility:

He took the turns of a motorbike
He took the kill of a deadly spider

And Scorpion was made.

Sam Tomlinson (9)
Hartsfield JMI School

Ape Began

(Based on 'Cat Began' by Andrew Matthews)

Ape began

He took the huff of the wolf
He took the loudness of the aeroplane
And made his voice

For his coat
He took the fluffiness of a silk sheet
He took the softness of the snow

For his walk
He took the noise of a building site
He took the squelch of the mud

For his eyes
He took that little speckle out of the sun
He took the shine of a new car

For his teeth
He took the sparkle of new glass
He took the toughness of the wrestler

And Ape was made.

Izzie Rodgers
Hartsfield JMI School

Leopard Began

(Based on 'Cat Began' by Andrew Matthews)

The leopard began:
He took the shape of the isosceles triangle
He took the hearing of a red deer
And he made his ears.

For his coat:
He took the spots of a boy with freckles
He took the black of the dark horse.

For his tail:
He took the log of a new tree
He took the waves of a smooth sea.

For his eyes:
He took the gold of the autumn corn
He took the sparkle of the silvery star.

For his nose:
He took the heart of the people
He took the wetness of a soaking puddle
And Leopard was made.

Erin Sunderland (10)
Hartsfield JMI School

Autumn

When autumn comes, leaves fall from the trees,
Brown, red and yellow leaves.
Trees sway from side to side,
Wind whistling,
Leaves crunching on the ground.
Branches rustle in the trees.
I can smell bonfires on Firework Night
And the smoke from the chimneys.

Callum Page
Hartsfield JMI School

Monkey Began

(Based on 'Cat Began' by Andrew Matthews)

Monkey began:
He took the sharpness of a knife
He took the whiteness of the snow
And made his teeth.

For his coat:
He took the brown of the boggy mud
He took the smoothness of a flat pebble.

For his tail:
He took the curl of a fossil
He took the length of a tree branch.

For his eyes:
He took the diamond of a ring
He took the gleam of the stars.

For his voice:
He took the cry of a wailing baby
He took the noise of the cheering crowd
And Monkey was made.

Callum McKenzie (9)
Hartsfield JMI School

Only In Autumn

I can see leaves diving to the floor like rockets.
I can hear the crunching sound of leaves.
I can smell damp leaves after showers, only in autumn.
I can feel the leaves as they blow in my face.
I can taste frosty wind as it blows on my tongue.
I can see, smell and taste the brown, burning bonfire.

Jake Fletcher (8)
Hartsfield JMI School

Golden Eagle Began

(Based on 'Cat Began' by Andrew Matthews)

Golden eagle began:
She took the sound of a nail on a blackboard
She took the loudness of the largest avalanche
And made her voice.

For her coat:
She took the smoothness of the pebble on the shore of the sea
She took the rare gold of the Queen's crown.

For her flight:
She took the pride of a king
She took the glide of the wind.

For her eyes:
She took the glow of a flaming candlestick
She took the colour of the greenest apple.

For her talons:
She took the clash of a dagger and silk
She took the grip of a boxer's fist
And Golden Eagle was made.

Kayla Ellis (10)
Hartsfield JMI School

Autumn Poem

I can see bare trees, fireworks in the air.
I can hear loud noises, especially fireworks.
I can smell smoke and gunpowder.
I can touch sparklers lighting up the air.
I can taste some warm, delicious apple pie
And some apple crumble.
Yum, yum, yum!

Rowan Godfrey
Hartsfield JMI School

Dog Began

(Based on 'Cat Began' by Andrew Matthews)

Dog began:
He took the twinkling of the smallest stars
He took the crunching of the sand
And made his voice

For his coat:
He took the softness of wool
He took the darkness of a turned off TV

For his walk:
He took the pride of the peacock
He took the silence of all the falling leaves

For his eyes:
He took the brightness of the sun
He took the blackness of a pencil lead

For his ears:
He took the flaps of the mirror on the OHP
He took the fur of a blanket
And Dog was made.

Amelia Ellis (9)
Hartsfield JMI School

Autumn Days

Autumn days when leaves fall off the tree
As slowly as a feather.
You can touch the leaves and the trees.
You can smell the bonfire
Where you can toast marshmallows.
Lovely leaves on the ground.
Shiny conkers falling from the trees like bombs.
Playing conker fights.

Harrison Bedford
Hartsfield JMI School

Wolf Began

(Based on 'Cat Began' by Andrew Matthews)

Wolf began:
He took the loudness of a jet turbine
He took the roughness of a grandad
And made his voice.

For his coat:
He took the softness of silk
He took the darkness of the night sky.

For his walk:
He took the slyness of a robber
He took the speed of a sports car.

For his eyes:
He took the colour of a burning flame
He took the glow of a dying light.

For his teeth:
He took the sharpness of a fine diamond
He took the jaggedness of broken glass
And Wolf was made.

Gregory Goddard (9)
Hartsfield JMI School

Autumn Is Coming

I can see the trees dying
And all the leaves falling off the branches and changing colour.
The cold, breezy wind blowing across the ground.

Autumn is here . . .

I can hear the sound of the crunchy leaves that people are
walking on
And all of the leaves crunched up.

Ryan Playle (9)
Hartsfield JMI School

Monkey Began

(Based on 'Cat Began' by Andrew Matthews)

Monkey began:
She took the echo of the caves
She took the cooing of the baby
And made her voice.

For her coat:
She took the softness of a teddy bear
She took the heat of a fire.

For her swing:
She took the height of the scaffolding
She took the soar of an aeroplane.

For her eyes:
She took the cuteness of the dog
She took the cheekiness of me.

For her energy:
She took the endlessness of water
She took the power of the gods
And Monkey was made.

Ryan Thompson (9)
Hartsfield JMI School

Autumn Days

Autumn is a time of year when the leaves start to fall like a waterfall.
People talking when they are walking.
People starting a fire and a singing choir.
I can touch the trees, can you?
I can smell smoke, can you smell it?
I'm stepping on the brown crunchy leaves.

Charlie Rodgers (8)
Hartsfield JMI School

Dog Began

(Based on 'Cat Began' by Andrew Matthews)

Dog began:
She took the sound of the breeze
She took the roughness of the Red Sea
And made her voice.

For her coat:
She took the softness of the clouds
She took the colour of snow.

For her walk:
She took the sound of the silent sky
She took the trot of a horse.

For her eyes:
She took the brightness of the moon
She took the sharpness of a diamond.

For her paws:
She took the roughness of rocks
She took the smoothness of pebbles
And Dog was made.

Emily Kelsall (10)
Hartsfield JMI School

Autumn Trees

The autumn trees are swishing like an elephant's trunk,
The wind is passing by like an electric car at top speed.

You can taste the cold air coming into your mouth
And out with steam.
You can hear the crunchy leaves
And see the yellow hot sun with the dull clouds.
You can touch the wet dew on the frosty fields
And the conkers falling on your head.

The autumn has gone.

Louis Mutter (8)
Hartsfield JMI School

Fox Began

(Based on 'Cat Began' by Andrew Matthews)

Fox began:
He took the silence of the stars
He took the swish of the water
And made his voice

For his coat:
He took the silkiness of a sheet
He took the softness of the snow

For his walk:
He took the speed of a snake
He took the camouflage of the leaves

For his eyes:
He took the yellow of the sun
He took the sparkle of the stars

For his teeth:
He took the point of a spike
He took the sharpness of ice
And Fox was made.

Steven Robinson
Hartsfield JMI School

Autumn Leaves

Autumn days are very windy.
Trees are swishing all about.
Yellow and green leaves on the trees.
The whistling wind in the air.
You taste the cold air coming in and out.
The leaves are going all about.
Leaves all so light,
Dark at night,
Windy whistles in the wind.

Victoria Lithgow (8)
Hartsfield JMI School

Autumn

Autumn days the conkers fall
Children pick them off the ground
Getting picked off the ground
Drilling holes in the conkers
Tying the string
Lovely leaves lying on the ground
Hear the crunching of the leaves
Smell the air
Feel the cool, cold air
Playing conker fights
Small conkers, big conkers
Conkers covered in leaves
Smell the cooking dinner
Picking up leaves
Look at the fireworks
Birds tweeting loudly
Birds making their nests
Crack the conker
Children begin to sing.

Alice Woodhouse (8)
Hartsfield JMI School

Autumn Days

Autumn is when the leaves fall,
Leaves start to crunch,
Conkers start to fall,
Start to smell roast dinner,
A burning smell of bonfires,
Crisps crunching like leaves,
Leaves floating through the air,
Cold air is starting to come,
Start to collect conkers,
Starting to have a Christmas feast,
Feathers starting to drift through the air.

Jake Dennis (8)
Hartsfield JMI School

Active Autumn

It's autumn time,
I can see leaves falling off the trees.
Everywhere I look, birds are flying south
And leaves are dancing around everywhere.

When I wake up,
The mornings are as cold
As a super deluxe freezer.
As I go outside,
I feel a frosty, crisp feeling in the air.

I look around
And I see scuttering squirrels.
The grass has turned a greeny grey colour.
I smell the smoky smell of set off fireworks.
I can hear the wind talking to me.
I just love active autumn!

Annie Ferrari (9)
Hartsfield JMI School

Autumn Days

Autumn days have come already.
The trees are not steady,
Trees are swaying side to side.
I can smell rotten leaves flying side to side,
The wild wind is blowing me away.
The leaves are turning into mud.
My hair is flying all over the place!

I can hear rustling leaves.
I can taste the breezy wind in my mouth.
The brown, crispy leaves I can see all over the place.
Now autumn is nearly over.
I just need to say, autumn rules!

Charles Draper (8)
Hartsfield JMI School

Caudipteryx Began

(Based on 'Cat Began' by Andrew Matthews)

Caudipteryx began:
She took the screech of the hawk
She took the loudness of the car
And made her voice.

For her coat:
She took the colours of the rainbow
She took the brightness of the torch.

For her walk:
She took the poshness of the Queen
She took the smoothness of a pebble.

For her eyes:
She took the sharpness of a knife
She took the pupil of a keyhole.

For her beak:
She took the orangeness of the sun
She took the pointiness of the diamond
And Caudipteryx was made.

James Hazzard (9)
Hartsfield JMI School

Autumn Poem

Autumn leaves, red, green, purple and pink.
Huge bangs as red, sparkling fireworks shoot into the sky.
Then the scary night of Hallowe'en.
That night ghosts, vampires, devils and skeletons appear.
You then hear the shout of 'Trick or treat?'
And in the windows you will see orange pumpkins with a
glowing candle.
This is autumn.

James Cook (8)
Hartsfield JMI School

Rabbit Began

(Based on 'Cat Began' by Andrew Matthews)

Rabbit began:
He took the crunch of the leaves,
He took the silence of a stone
And made his voice.

For his coat:
He took the softness of the clouds
He took the warmness of fur.

For his walk:
He took the speed of the tiger
He took the hop of a pogo stick.

For his eyes:
He took the sparkle of the stars
He took the glow of the lava lamp.

For his hop:
He took the bounce of a ball
He took the height of a tower
And Rabbit was made.

Caprice Brookes
Hartsfield JMI School

Autumn Days

In autumn I can see brown leaves
Falling off the trees and dying.
I can see the leaves flying like aeroplanes
And dancing like fairies as well.

I can hear crunching of crunchy leaves
And birds flapping their wings,
Flying to the south.
I can smell smoke from bonfires
And soggy leaves.

Owen Marvell
Hartsfield JMI School

Snake Began

(Based on 'Cat Began' by Andrew Matthews)

Snake began:
She took the hiss of the angry goose
She took the hardness of hail
And made her voice.

For her skin:
She took the slenderness of a twig
She took the glossiness of the diamond.

For her slither:
She took the movement of a swimmer
She took the gracefulness of the Queen.

For her eyes:
She took the shimmer of topaz
She took the blackness of tunnels.

For her heart:
She took the sneakiness of a thief
She took the coldness of the winter
And Snake was made.

Jessica Farey (9)
Hartsfield JMI School

Autumn Poem

Smoke from banging red rockets.
I can smell burning candles from pumpkins.
I can taste sweets from Hallowe'en, pumpkins and apple pie.
Buckets full of sweets.
Autumn is like a conker shell cracking open.
Ruby-red rockets rise right up.
Candy crackling and crisp.
Hedgehogs hibernate happily.

Charlotte Duke (8)
Hartsfield JMI School

Dog Began

(Based on 'Cat Began' by Andrew Matthews)

Dog began:
She took the howling of the wind
She took the screeching of a blackboard
And made her voice.

For her coat:
She took the colour of a branch
She took the whiteness of snow.

For her walk:
She took the silence of stars
She took the madness of a monkey.

For her eyes:
She took the green of the grass
She took the black of the night.

For her body:
She took the strength of a rock
She took the shape of the biggest water bottle
And Dog was made.

Georgina Watson
Hartsfield JMI School

It's Hallowe'en

Autumn time is finally here
It's time for Hallowe'en!
It's Hallowe'en! It's Hallowe'en!
People shouting, 'Trick or treat?'
Kids asking for candy
Children dressing up for Hallowe'en
Pumpkins with candles in
Next year there might be even more horror.

Ravannah Liddar (8)
Hartsfield JMI School

Snake Began

(Based on 'Cat Began' by Andrew Matthews)

Snake began:
He took the rustling of bushes
He took the quietness of stones in a desert
And made his voice.

For his coat:
He took the smoothness of a moray eel from the darkest sea
He took the dryness of the longest beach.

For his slither:
He took the slidyness of a drop slide
He took the stretchiness of a bungee-jumping rope.

For his eyes:
He took the flame of the blazing sun
He took the water of the sea.

For his fangs:
He took the point of a knife
He took the whiteness of a whiteboard
And Snake was made.

Nathan Gilbert (9)
Hartsfield JMI School

Autumn Poem

Red rockets in the sky going high. *Bang!*
Sparklers going high and low in the wind.
Bonfire smoke blows side to side in the wind.
Lights bright and beautiful.

Che Mabert
Hartsfield JMI School

Dog Began

(Based on 'Cat Began' by Andrew Matthews)

Dog began:
She took the roughness of the midnight sea
She took the sound of the breeze
And made her voice.

For her coat:
She took the softness of clouds
She took the whiteness of snow.

For her walk:
She took the snapping of a falling branch
She took the trot of the horse.

For her eyes:
She took the glitter of the stars
She took the brightness of the brightest light.

For her ears:
She took the roundness of the football
She took the pointiness of the pencil
And Dog was made.

Megan Green (9)
Hartsfield JMI School

Autumn

Red, ruby rockets rising
Chocolate-coloured conkers cracking
Bonfires banging, breaking bark
These remind me of autumn.

Will Bell (8)
Hartsfield JMI School

Hamster Began

(Based on 'Cat Began' by Andrew Matthews)

Hamster began:
He took the squeak of wet shoes
And made his voice.

For his coat:
He took the colour of snow
He took the softness of cat hair.

For his walk:
He took the speed of bikes.

For his eyes:
He took the size of a bead
He took the blackness of the night sky.

For his ears:
He took the pointiness of elf ears
And Hamster was made.

Kathryn Bingham (9)
Hartsfield JMI School

Autumn

Autumn leaves, red and brown,
Smoke from the fire
And children dressed in costumes for Hallowe'en
And pumpkins with candles in.

Fireworks going off,
The sound of cracking conkers
And the wind whistling in my ear.

I can smell the fire on Bonfire Night
And fireworks.
I can taste toffee apple, pumpkin pie,
Apple pie and roasted marshmallows.

Max Walsh (9)
Hartsfield JMI School

Hedgehog Began

(Based on 'Cat Began' by Andrew Matthews)

Hedgehog began:
He took the spikes of the hairbrush
He took the timidness of the dormouse.

For his coat:
He took the brown of the tree bark
He took the soft tummy of the feathers from a bird.

For his walk:
He took the slowness of the sky floating by
He took the movement of the rolling pin.

For his eyes:
He took the blackness of the night sky
He took the roundness of the ball.

For his voice:
He took the softness of the late night
He took the shuffle of the breeze
And Hedgehog was made.

Meghan Porter (9)
Hartsfield JMI School

Autumn Days

Autumn days,
Leaves are falling,
The day is dawning,
Trees are waving in the wind,
Leaves are swirling like a circle.

Bonfires smelling,
Fireworks shooting in the sky,
Days are getting shorter by the second,
Grass is getting browner,
Brown leaves, yellow leaves, red leaves, green leaves,
But they're all the same leaves.

David Stevenson (8)
Hartsfield JMI School

Tiger Began

(Based on 'Cat Began' by Andrew Matthews)

Tiger began:
She took the racket of the microphone
She took the eruption of the volcano
And made her voice.

For her coat:
She took the silkiness of a sheet
She took the point of a thorn.

For her walk:
She took the speed of a jet
She took the flexibility of a cheetah.

For her eyes:
She took the shine of the stars
She took the black of the dark night.

For her teeth:
She took the sharpness of ice
She took the point of the arrow
And Tiger was made.

Courtney Nash
Hartsfield JMI School

Autumn Poem

Sparklers spinning in the sky
Crunchy leaves crunching as you walk by
Trees swaying in the sky
Ruby-red rockets shooting up in the sky
People shouting, 'Trick or treat?'
Smell those apple pies
Autumn is the best.

Sophie Bosworth (8)
Hartsfield JMI School

Red Panda Began

(Based on 'Cat Began' by Andrew Matthews)

Red panda began:
He took the quietness of the trees
He took the softness of the clouds
And made his voice.

For his coat:
He took the red of the heart
He took the pattern of the stripe.

For his walk:
He took the trot of the horse
He took the sweetness of the wind.

For his eyes:
He took the colour of the branches
He took the sparkle of night.

For his body:
He took the shape of the leaf
He took the shine of the sun
And Red Panda was made.

Juliet Oliver (9)
Hartsfield JMI School

Autumn Poem

A utumn comes before winter
U p, up the leaves go
'T rick or treat?' the children say
U mbrellas turning inside out
M ums cooking feasts
N o one hates autumn.

Jordan Robinson
Hartsfield JMI School

Autumn Season

Autumn days are coming,
Everybody is having fun.
Crunching in the lovely leaves
In the cool breeze.

Trees are swishing, swishing, swishing,
Like they're playing games.
Leaves are swirling, swirling, swirling,
Like they are dancing.

I can hear fireworks
And I can see they are bursting to all the colours of the rainbow.
I can smell a bonfire
And I can hear it is crackling like fire in your fireplace.

I can hear the wind whistling
And I can see the leaves changing to different colours.
Leaves as brown as chocolate or as red as flames,
As yellow as the sun or as orange as a flower.
The wind is blowing hard like a tornado has struck.

Autumn is the best.

Lucy Seaton
Hartsfield JMI School

Autumn

The leaves falling down and not making a sound
The crunchy leaves as I walk through them
Crunchy, curly leaves
The smell of fireworks
Pretty rockets, perfect purple and pink
Chocolate-coated coconut, lovely and crunchy
Munching as I walk along.

Katie Shoobert (8)
Hartsfield JMI School

Hamster Began

(Based on 'Cat Began' by Andrew Matthews)

Hamster began:
She took the snapping of breaking branches
She took the roughness of a leaf
And made her voice.

For her coat:
She took the softness of the sand
She took the smoothness of a curtain.

For her walk:
She took the quietness of the cat
She took the slowness of a boat.

For her eyes:
She took the sparkle of fire
She took the glow of the sun.

For her nose:
She took the flatness of a button
She took the pinkness of a love heart
And Hamster was made.

Callum Duffy (9)
Hartsfield JMI School

Autumn Poem

Children standing on the doorstep waiting to jump out
I hear the bonfire just lit
I can smell the gunpowder in the fireworks
I hear children saying, 'Trick or treat?'
I can touch the specks of the sparks
There are busy bangers buzzing by.

Louie Welch (8)
Hartsfield JMI School

Goldfish Began

(Based on 'Cat Began' by Andrew Matthews)

Goldfish began:
He took the twinkling of the stars
He took the bubbles from the washing up liquid
And made his voice.

For his coat:
He took the smoothness of glass
He took the scales of a snake.

For his swim:
He took the slowness of the second-hand clock
He took the sound from the waterfall.

For his eyes:
He took the blackness from the sky for his pupil
He took the paleness of a grey sky.

For his fins:
He took the thinness of a sheet
He took the wetness of a float in water
And Goldfish was made.

Jody Margetson (9)
Hartsfield JMI School

Things About Autumn

I can see the tree swaying side to side
And the leaves falling from the trees.
I can hear leaves crunching on the ground
And wind whistling.
I can smell smoke from the chimneys.
I can taste marshmallows from the burning bonfire.
I can touch leaves from the trees.

Mathew Brown (8)
Hartsfield JMI School

Tiger Began

(Based on 'Cat Began' by Andrew Matthews)

Tiger began:
He took the loud call of the trumpet
He took the crashing of the sea
And made his voice.

For his coat:
He took the softness of velvet
He took the amazing orange of a burning flame.

For his walk:
He took the smoothness of moving water
He took the slyness of the fox.

For his eyes:
He took the blinding glare of the sun
He took the sparkle of a diamond.

For his teeth:
He took the shape of a triangle
He took the sharpness of a knife
And Tiger was made.

Laura Martin (10)
Hartsfield JMI School

Autumn

You can see leaves in autumn
Rustling leaves on the ground
The wind is whistling
You can smell the hot bonfire
Bark on the hard and lumpy tree
Hard, hot bread boiling like an oven.

Crunchy leaves
Fresh, chilly air
Rough tree trunks
Singing birds with their wings spread.

Emily Arnold (8)
Hartsfield JMI School

Crocodile Began

(Based on 'Cat Began' by Andrew Matthews)

Crocodile began.
He took the sharpness of a farmer's scythe
He took the white from a polar bear's fur
And made his teeth.

For his skin:
He took the strength of a raging hog
He took the green of the prickly gorse bush.

For his walk:
He took the plodding of the elephant
He took the patience of a snake on a hunt.

For his eyes:
He took the orange of a burning fire
He took the darkness of the night sky.

For his tail:
He took the length of the boa constrictor
He took the strength of a roaring lion
And Crocodile was made.

Robert Brierley (9)
Hartsfield JMI School

Snake Began

(Based on 'Cat Began' by Andrew Matthews)

Snake began:
He took the flicker of the speedy lizard
And took the redness of the fire
And made his tongue.

For his skin:
He took the patterns of the rainbow
He took the toughness of the rock.

For his fangs:
He took the sharpness of the needle
He took the poison of the ivy.

For his eyes:
He took the awareness of the eagle
He took the piercing of the tack.

For his body:
He took the links of the chain
And took the flexibility of a gymnast
And Snake was made.

Max Dewing (10)
Hartsfield JMI School

Rabbit Began

(Based on 'Cat Began' by Andrew Matthews)

Rabbit began:
She took the brown of the boring bark
She took the black of the night sky
And made her colour.

For her teeth:
She took the sharpness of the broken glass
She took the glossiness of the polished boot.

For her bounce:
She took the hop of the happy kangaroo
She took the distance of the flying hoverfly.

For her eyes:
She took the blue of the beautiful sky
She took the sparkle of the night stars.

For her tail:
She took the fluffiness of the cosy cotton wool
She took the whiteness of the coldest snow
And Rabbit was made.

Alana Sullivan
Hartsfield JMI School

Giraffe Began

(Based on 'Cat Began' by Andrew Matthews)

Giraffe began:
She took the yellow of the brightest buttercup
She took the black of the darkest rain cloud
And made her colour.

For her body:
She took the length of the lamp post
She took the diameter of a water tank.

For her walk:
She took the legs of the table leg
She took the level of the spirit level.

For her eyes:
She took the white of a summer's cloud
She took the brown of a chocolate bar.

For her ears:
She took the softness of the fluffy pillow
She took the length of a daffodil
And Giraffe was made.

Matthew Dyne (9)
Hartsfield JMI School

Monkey Began

(Based on 'Cat Began' by Andrew Matthews)

Monkey began:
He took the brownness of the mud
He took the sharpness of the blade
And made his feet.

For his coat:
He took the brownness of the tree trunk
He took the smoothness of the silk.

For his personality:
He took the cheekiness of the boy
He took the cleverness of the scientist.

For his tail:
He took the curliness of a girl's hair
He took the length of the road.

For his eyes:
He took the brightness of the moon
He took the green of the emeralds
And Monkey was made.

Holly Hayes (10)
Hartsfield JMI School

Tiger Began

(Based on 'Cat Began' by Andrew Matthews)

Tiger began:
She took the roar from a child screaming
She took the growling from the angry dog.

For her coat:
She took the orange of the bright rose
She took the cotton of the new cloth.

For her walk:
She took the proudness of the oldest oak tree.

For her paws:
She took the shape of the rose petals.

For her eyes:
She took the orange from the whole bricks
She took the brown from the beautiful bark.

For her teeth:
She took the sharpness from the shiniest metal
She took the dirt from the leftover plates.

Daisy Flynn (9)
Hartsfield JMI School

Spider Began

(Based on 'Cat Began' by Andrew Matthews)

Spider began:
He took the poison of the cobra
He took the whisper of the wind
And made his voice.

For his coat:
He took the darkness of midnight
He took the smoothness of the silk worm.

For his walk:
He took the speed of the cheetah
He took the slyness of the fox.

For his eyes:
He took the red of blood
He took the shape of the round moon.

For his legs:
He took the sticks of the oak tree
He took the hair of the witch's broom
And Spider was made.

Callum Dungey (9)
Hartsfield JMI School

Crocodile Began

(Based on 'Cat Began' by Andrew Matthews)

Crocodile began:
He took the roaring of the angry lion
He took the howling of the blowing wind
And made his voice.

For his skin:
He took the roughness of a building brick
He took the greenness of the long grass
He took the stiffness of old wood.

For his teeth:
He took the sharpness of a needle
He took the point of the eagle's claw.

For his eyes:
He took the yellow of the beach sand
He took the shadows of the buildings.

For his tail:
He took the length of an exotic tree
He took the strength of five rhinos
And Crocodile was made.

Alex Smith (9)
Hartsfield JMI School

Monkey Began

(Based on 'Cat Began' by Andrew Matthews)

Monkey began:
She took hair from the cow
She took smoothness from the snow
And made her coat.

For her sound:
She took the squeak from the mouse
She took the volume from the scream.

For her moves:
She took the speed from the cheetah
She took the swaying from the trees.

For her eyes:
She took the blueness from the summer sky
She took the sparkle of a diamond.

For her size:
She took the smoothness from the ant
She took size from the mouse
And that made Monkey.

Eleanor Wase
Hartsfield JMI School

Dog Began

(Based on 'Cat Began' by Andrew Matthews)

Dog began:
He took the growl of a furious tiger
He took the teeth of a lion
And made his voice.

For his coat:
He took the fur of the giraffe
He took the brown of the chestnut horse.

For his walk:
He took the pace of the leopard
He took the paws of the panther.

For his eyes:
He took the stare of the owl
He took the blue of the summer sky.

For his claws:
He took the talons of the wolf
He took the sharpness of the cheetah's teeth
And Dog was made.

Georgina Crowther (9)
Hartsfield JMI School

Dog Began

(Based on 'Cat Began' by Andrew Matthews)

Dog began:
He took the speed of the cheetah
He took the steadiness of the longest day
And made his walk.

For his coat:
He took the softness of a pillow
He took the colour of the tree bark.

For his body:
He took the size of the river rocks
He took the white of the tiger.

For his eyes:
He took the sharpness of a sniper's aim
He took the ears of a sensor.

For his voice:
He took the howling of a wolf
He took the gentle rustle of a bush
And Dog was made.

Tom Kendle (9)
Hartsfield JMI School

Rabbit Began

(Based on 'Cat Began' by Andrew Matthews)

Rabbit began:
She took the fluffiness of the duckling
She took the sensitivity of the dog.

For her coat:
She took the greyness of the cloud in winter
She took the softness of a feather.

For her speed:
She took the bounce of the kangaroo
She took the fastness of the wasp.

For her eyes:
She took the bark from the trees
She took the brownness of the mud.

For her body:
She took the size of the big pencil case
She took the fatness of the elephant
And Rabbit was made.

Francesca Rowley (9)
Hartsfield JMI School

Fish Began

(Based on 'Cat Began' by Andrew Matthews)

Fish began:
She took the water from the tap
She took the plants from the pet shop
And made her habitat.

For her coat:
She took the brightest flame for her orange coat
She took the blue from the brightest sky
And made her coat.

She took the bright blue of the sea
She took the roundness of a ring
And made her eyes.

She took the quietness of a mouse
And the gentleness of the wind
And made her voice.

She took the size of the smallest potato
And took the speed of a fast worm
And Fish was made.

Ellie Welch (9)
Hartsfield JMI School

Dog Began

(Based on 'Cat Began' by Andrew Matthews)

Dog began:
He took the banging of the wooden stair for his bark.

He took the wetness of the pond and made his nose.

For his coat he took the smoothness of the moon.
He took the marks of a tiger.

For his walk he took the speed of the wind.
He took the clumsiness of a one-legged hamster.

For his eyes he took the brownness of the mud.
He took the roundness of a circle.

For his ears he took the point of a claw.
He took the softness of a rug . . .

And Dog was made.

Sophie Weston (9)
Hartsfield JMI School

The World I Would Like To Live In . . .

Is full of delicious fruit
Mangos full of ripe juice
Pineapples as bright as the sun
Apples as green as the grass
Bananas waiting to be picked
Tomatoes hanging like red tulips
The air is filled with the sweetest scent
I love my island.

James Ivell (7)
How Wood School

The World I Would Like To Live In

Everyone would have a Nintendo Wii or what about a PS3?
Given a flatscreen TV or would you like a new phone?
Look at all these nice things, like luscious plain monster fields
for all the wildlife to gather like a swarm of bees.
Next door to all that wildlife would be some huge giant, gigantic
or some colossal mansions for the humans.
There would also be no bills or taxes, so everyone would be free
from a life sentence in a deep, dark dungeon.

All the people would be rich like never before, just the same
feeling as Peter Pan swooping you off to Neverland.
We would all have amazing jobs that some of us couldn't think
of even in our wildest dreams.
Every country would be as healthy as a child's thoughts on
Christmas Day.
There would be no pollution in the atmosphere, like an answered
prayer to God.
There would be a law on recycling.

Clark Hodsdon (11)
How Wood School

The World I Would Like To Live In

Peace is here, no racist wars,
There is only love.
No jealousy or crime
And no extinction.

Peace and love will fill the land,
With liking and learning.
We use gas lamps,
There's no TV.
There's gallons of laughter, ho, ho, hee, hee,
There's fields of wheat like a golden bedsheet.
This is the world I'd like to live in.

Andrew Urquhart (10)
How Wood School

The World I Would Like To Live In . . .

Is full of bats that hang
Like stones from the ceiling.
About to fall.
Using radar to find creepy insects.
Their wings make a swoosh.
Everytime they flap.
Their big ears look like a bit of beef.
Be not afraid . . .

Freddie Wernham (7)
How Wood School

The World I Would Like To Live In

The world is full of food
The world is full of smells
All the beautiful fruits
Mango as green as grass
Grapes as black as olives
Apples as round as a ball
Strawberries as red as blood
The world is full of peaches
Soft and juicy, runny and sweet.

Shakil Chowdhury (8)
How Wood School

The World I Would Like To Live In

An island surrounded by water
Blue as the sky on a hot summer's day
Fish scales as beautiful as stars in the sky
Dolphins jump out of water
Like women dancing with jewels round their necks
Water sloshes against the beach
That's how the world will be for me.

Annabel Clarke (8)
How Wood School

The World I Would Like To Live In

My world would have green luscious grass reaching over the land,
Sunset would shine its warm glow at night,
At dawn, everything fresh and new with excitement,
Flowers with their golden shine, spreading over the fields,
Peace would be everywhere with no need for war,
Motorways and cars wouldn't exist, but just think of the place to be and land there!
People would be smart, but not think themselves better than others,
There would be no need for money, everything can run free!
Everyone feels safe and proud to be different,
At night the moon and stars come out to play and dance all night,
Birds in the trees singing as happy as can be,
Trees bold and as colossal as a giraffe,
Landscapes and islands so picturesque,
Lands wide and open,
Islands with warm sand beneath my feet.

Gemma Kaur-Brown (10)
How Wood School

The World I Would Like To Live In

Dogs are howling at the postman like a beast growling at a mouse
Horses galloping round all day long
Watching the sunset on the beach, getting very hot
Lovely growing flowers in every field
Water melons getting cut up all day long
No global warming so the Earth is healthier
Children playing in the field
Let's all go and have some fun
Hear Mum shout, 'Time for dinner.'

Emily Leech (10)
How Wood School

The World I Would Like To Live In

This world is black, silent, there's nobody but me.
Then appears a creamy yellow, just bright enough for the eye to see.
What's that I see? So beautiful, yet still, it's a charm bracelet, dainty
little thing.
I also see an amber ring.

This world is a creamy yellow, silent but somehow not the same
as before!
Oh my, a lamp post pointing to the lane that will end up at the
bottom of my future house's door.
What's that I hear? It's the most beautiful sound, it's a music
box's tune.
I look up, there's a baby-blue moon.

This world is a creamy yellow with a baby-blue moon with a music
box tune.
What's that I hear? A soft whinny from a foal who will appear soon!
What's that I smell? Talcum powder on my cat who has just run by.
What's that I hear? My grandad's sigh.

This world is now colourful and freshly scented.
It's a lovely atmosphere too.
What's that smell? It's my brother's shampoo.
What's that colour? So soothingly soft, it's rosy-pink.
What's that smell? It's my mum's lavender perfume sitting beside
the sink.

Emily Smith (9)
How Wood School

The World I Would Like To Live In

Beautiful, multicoloured gardens fill the land like a rainbow carpet.
Thousands of puppies jumping around like a Mexican wave.
Open fields filled with white blossoms, like a snowy blanket.
Slow rain falling with a pitter-patter, like a little ant scuttling along.

William Webster (10)
How Wood School

The World I Would Like To Live In

Beautiful countryside everywhere, filling the land like buildings.
The plants will be healthy because there will be no pollution in the air.
Healthy food that tastes so tasty, to fill up my belly when I'm hungry.
Good weather, no floods or tornados and snow in the winter on
Christmas Day.

Everyone is friends, playing together like cheerful kittens,
So there will be no bullies if everyone is a smiling friend.
As we are friends, we share our perfect world together.

Rachel Quarterman (10)
How Wood School

The World I Would Like To Live In

Rabbits hopping around eating luscious emerald-green grass,
Squirrels climbing trees and collecting their chocolatey-brown
chestnuts,
Butterflies are planes, flying through the air,
In the daisy-covered field where the bugs live happily under
the flowers,
But the world is at peace, like a tree waving in the wind.

Samuel Clarke (10)
How Wood School

The World I Would Like To Live In

The people of the world would be kind to everyone,
Never fight, never do a crime,
There would be no extinctions, like as we say bye-bye,
My Chemical Romance will always play, booming us away,
Wolves and cats will be everywhere, like they own the planet,
All the chocolate will be turned healthy, but still have a lovely taste,
It would be impossible to have bullies, they would have evaporated.

Jordan Miller (10)
How Wood School

The World I Would Like To Live In

A bright sunset falling every evening like a light going out.
There would be less pollution and more recycling.
Small, soft raindrops dripping from the sky.
I would like people to ride harmless horses.
There would be sandy horse tracks and less roads.
There could be wild animals everywhere, with birds flying in the air.
All the people would be kind and thoughtful.
Flowers everywhere, like a carpet beneath your feet.

Emily Colbourne (11)
How Wood School

The World I Would Like To Live In

In my world I can see three colours emerge from the misty clouds.
The colours are sapphire-blue, sandy orange and bright yellow.
I can hear a lovely guitar playing peacefully,
A car revving and a football crowd singing.
I can smell aftershave and chocolate and bacon coming from a house.
Two objects appear in front of me,
A football and a treasure chest.
I see a signpost pointing to home.

Lewis Hough (9)
How Wood School

The World I Would Like To Live In

Roses scattered like salt over spicy, red chilli con carne,
Chocolate and books grow on trees like juicy fruit,
There shall be no crime and no war,
All there is is a carpet of tortoises,
There is no pollution, just a blanket of clean, fresh air,
All the people are kind, friendly and harmless,
Money doesn't exist - everything is free.

Tyler Town (10)
How Wood School

The World I Would Like To Live In

As I am walking along, I see the colour sea-blue,
Then I smell the flavour vanilla,
Also I see a sign pointing to home.
Next, out of nowhere, I hear my dad's voice in the breeze.

As I am walking along, I get a whiff of melted chocolate,
And then I see the colour grass-green.
Also I see my teddy bear that I got when I was a baby.
Next I see a sign pointing to my mum's house.
Last I smell my mum's perfume.

As I am walking along, I see the colour midnight-black,
Then I see a crowd of people singing happily.
Next I smell hot chocolate from the kettle.
Last, I see a sign pointing to an Indian sunset.

Billy Grace (9)
How Wood School

The World I Would Like To Live In

Bright green, jewelled grass filling the land
Warm, fresh air blowing through my hair
Lovely orange sunsets ending every good day
Pretty flowers filling all the fields
Peace and quiet on the seashore
Kindness to animals and people - no one gets hurt
Kittens mewing like a small lamb
Puppies barking like a lost cub
No bullies hurting people like a tiger killing its prey
No bombs blowing up buildings and destroying everything
No stabbing making things red like a ruby
No pollution filling the blue sky
No guns shooting people who are innocent.

Natasha Ross (10)
How Wood School

The World I Would Like To Live In

Jogging along a misty street,
Colours scattered around my feet,
Grassy-green and baby-blue,
I can see blood-red too.
These sounds, a pony whinnying,
Mum's calm voice whispering kindly,
Tiny twitching and scattering coming from delicate golden hamsters.
A few objects I can see,
One bay pony glaring at me,
Another person like me, but taller and older,
Definitely bigger and definitely bolder.
Beautiful smells of ponies' hay, wafting from a stable,
Sweet smell of chocolate, waiting on the table.
Lastly, a signpost pointing to a beautiful country farmhouse,
Surrounded by trees and flowers,
I expect the farmer must work for hours.

Ella Molloy (9)
How Wood School

The World I Would Like To Live In

Smiley stuff fills the shelves, like a field of yellow flowers.
Everyone is happy and smiley and never sad or lonely.
Cars are run by batteries, not petrol.
There are less cars on the road and no lorries to pollute the air.
No more Internet cyber bullying, everyone is kind.
All websites are safe and don't leave a virus on your computer.
More websites like 'Club Penguin', with excellent security.
No more teenage gangs in London, killing every innocent person they see.
No playground bullies, instead a swarm of kind people.
No more witch teachers telling you off for nothing.

Sarah Ivell (11)
How Wood School

The World I'd Like To Live In

I see in front of me a pale blue, tweeting bird tweeting me a tune.
I see in front of me a lavender baby violet smelling like a dream.
I see in front of me a vanilla-scented candle, sitting on top of a
sweet-smelling, crackling fire.
I see below me crisp conkers lying on the ground.
I see in front of me a horse and foal grooming each other.
I hear the faint sound of a violin in the background.
I see a gorgeous little kitten lying beside me as I dream about the
world I'd like to live in.
I hear the soft whining of the foal I've always dreamed of.

Taylor Francis (9)
How Wood School

The World I'd Like To Live In

As I walk through the clouds
I'm surrounded by three colours
Ruby-red, sapphire-blue and orange sunset.
As I walk through the misty clouds
I hear three amazing sounds
Swish, sway, do-da, do-da and the sound of vroom, vroom.
As I walk through the clouds
I smell the beautiful scent of flowers, roses, daffodils and poppies.

Daniel Brazier (9)
How Wood School

The World I Would Like To Live In

The world I would like to live in would be bright
The sea would be baby-blue
You would be yellow
There would be lots of animals coming up to you
Making lots of noise
There would be a sign pointing towards home.

Jake Grace (9)
How Wood School

The World I Would Like To Live In

The world is full of sounds
The ocean that glimmers all day long
The noisy lions passing by the old, rusty trees
The whistling of birds that glide through the air that stares at the glazing sun

Leaves float in the soft, calm air
Clouds shaped like my favourite animals
Gentle drums beat up above
Couples kiss in the high hilltops
Families clap in the darkness.

Louisa Rosato (8)
How Wood School

The World I'd Like To Live In

Chocolate melted in the grass,
Puppies pouncing like a leopard in the jungle,
Roses popping through the space,
Tortoises walking in slow motion,
Open air breathes through my clothes.

I love to play with the toys,
Play equipment, oh so very tall,
Bouncy castles yellow and green.

Hannah Cole (10)
How Wood School

The World I Would Like To Live In

Sunsets filling the sky of evening air,
Green grass spreading everywhere like the spider's eight legs,
Water lilies in every small pond to show happiness in the world,
Monkeys jumping from tree to tree searching for bananas in the rainforest,
Everyone can recycle to have less pollution in the world.

Gabby Wroe (10)
How Wood School

The World I'd Like To Live In

I walk and see in front of me
A guitar strumming in the sunlight
Such a wonderful, crispy white
The scent of lavender that I found
Leaves falling to the ground

Birds making such a sweet tune
My lovely perfume
A pale blue above my head
Leaves now resting, creating a mound

A harp making a glorious tune
The violet colour darkening the sky
A dog panting next to me
The smell of a candle under my feet
Now the vast trees.

Charlotte Springle (9)
How Wood School

The World I'd Like To Live In

This is a weird world that I have seen
But first I see a grassy-green
Then I see a shiny yellow
After a while a fiery red
Then I hear the call of the dead
Then I hear the chime of bells
That is when I get the scent of smells
At first I smell some food
Then I smell lavender in a pot
That is when I see a shiny red diamond shining in my eyes
An old piece of metal
I pick them up and put them in my pocket
Then I see what I am waiting for
It is the signpost pointing to home.

Robert Simpson (9)
How Wood School

The World I'd Like To Live In

The world is full of big animals
Snakes slither along the cold, stony ground
Bright, spotty leopards hunt for meat
Black, camouflaged scorpions, as poisonous as a cobra
The antelopes are jumping higher than the highest trees

The animals like grizzly bears sleeping and snoring
Slithery, slimy tree snakes slithering up trees
Rhinos charging at thick coconut trees
Monkeys swinging in the autumn leaves

The crocodiles will not harm a single soul
Frogs swimming in the fresh water
Minibeasts climbing trees
Tasmanian devils chasing each other
Crabs creeping through the rock pools
Starfish stick to the rough, seaweedy rocks
Eels as long as a tree trunk
Fish hiding in coral at the bottom of the sea
The sharks are my friends and will not harm you
Owls swooping down for fresh worms.

Tommy Colbourne (8)
How Wood School

The World I Would Like To Live In

The world is full of beautiful, calm birds
A great tit as blue as the wavy sea
A swan as white as lovely soft snow
A heron as grey as black storm clouds

The world is full of birds
The robin shines in the bright moonlight
The blue tit that smells like the salty sea
The lovely magpie that pecks for food
Flamingos that always stand in the middle of a lake.

Jade Scott (8)
How Wood School

The World I Would Like To Live In

The world is full of jewels
Sapphires blue
Like the sky above us
Diamonds silver
Like shimmering stars
Rubies red
Like scented roses
All of these are shiny and beautiful

The world is full of sea creatures
Crabs peach
Like a peach flower
Sea horses blue
Like the silky, salty ocean
Fish silver
Like yummy, healthy food
All of these are my favourite sea creatures.

Morgan Henry (8)
How Wood School

The World I Would Like To Live In

The world is full of excitement
Shimmering pearls that glimmer in the sunlight
Bouncing bunnies that hop along the silky sand
Juicy strawberries that make you want to eat them.

The world is full of happiness
Giggling children that skip along happily
Chattering teenagers walking to Scouts
Muttering, moaning mums who are fed up
Daydreaming dads that are on the way to the pub
Everyone is happy
What better world can you wish for?
This is the life.

Ellie Neil (8)
How Wood School

The World I Would Like To Live In

The world is full of water
That falls off the clean stones all day long.
The pale blue water sways around in the salty sea.
Starfish that stick to the hard edge of the rock pool,
Whales squirt water as I sail past.

The world is full of leaves
That fall from autumn trees.
Red, yellow or green leaves.
When I walk past I hear a rustle,
As they float as gently as a blanket.

The world is full of flowers
That are scented with perfume.
Pink, blue, white or red, they still smell great.
As they poke up, you see pretty petals,
Red roses that smell of love.

The world is full of birds
That sing all day long.
As trees sway in the breeze,
You say to yourself -
What better world could you wish for?

Amy Brunton (8)
How Wood School

The World I Would Like To Live In

The world is full of jewels
That glimmer in the dark
A moonstone as blue as a glittery, sparkly sea
The sunstone is like a pounding sun
The diamonds and rubies are like two sparkling jewels
The pink mineral is like a blooming flower
The chaos emerald is like the tall, green grass
The reflecting jewels reflect your sparkling face.

Yasmin Arron-Gonzalez (8)
How Wood School

The World I'd Like To Live In

In my dazzling, perfect world there is a newborn baby
With the most beautiful blue eyes.
I wish I could still hear my grandpa just saying hi!

I smell the waft of a chocolate cake whizzing straight past,
An adorable light blue, so calm and vast.

A fluffy white and a rosy red,
Oh, how I wish I could never go to bed!

I look all around and guess what I see?
A cute little kitten looking up at me.

The scent of roses,
My mum and dad,
To stay in this world, it makes me feel glad.

If you like my perfect world,
Come and visit:
My cute little kitten,
The scent of roses,
An adorable blue,
A chocolate cake,
Your mum and dad,
It'll all make you glad!

Maisie Mannering (9)
How Wood School

The World I'd Like To Live In

The sky is a baby-blue
The sun is like sand on a beach
A dark black car
The grass is a gorgeous green
It shines in the sunshine
I can smell some apple pie
My nan's apple pie
I love my nan's apple pie.
So nice.

Gordon Strong (9)
How Wood School

The World I Would Like To Live In

The world is full of nature
The grass glimmers in the sunlight
The birds sing in the autumn trees
The leaves fall off the tall trees
Rain splashes at the flowers
Rainbows lighten the sky with all the rainbow colours
Sunflowers glimmer in the sparkling, shiny sun

The world is full of colour
Colours of red, like burning fire
Colours of yellow, like the glowing sun
Colours of green, like the long, high grass
Colours of everything
There are colours everywhere
Is this the best world?

Ken Lee (8)
How Wood School

The World I'd Like To Live In

The world is full of fruit trees
Strawberries shine in the beating sun
Coconuts swaying in the trees
Bananas squish and squash in my mouth as I chew them
Oranges as orange as the flaming hot sun
Lemons rolling around as they fall onto the hot ground
Water melons splitting as they hit the ground

The world is full of waving water
Spiky sharks trying to bite your feet
Dolphins and whales dive backwards and forwards
Shiny shells shine through the water
Then you come home to relax
After a great day on the water.

Charley Lawrence (8)
How Wood School

The World I'd Like To Live In

The world is full of delicious fruit
Mango-orange like the huge hot sun
A peach like an edible crab
Oranges like the crispy autumn leaves
Strawberries squashy and ready to eat
Coconuts fall off trees
Giving everybody fresh milk to keep for the winter
Yummy!

The world is full of scented flowers
The flowers dance in the light of the moon
The roses scent the air around me
The lovely oranges falling off the orange trees
Limes sway in the soft, calm sea

The world is full of glimmering jewels
A red ruby like a beautiful rose that lights up the sky
A moonstone as precious as your loving family
The tune of jewels splashing in the silky ocean.

Fiona Moignard (8)
How Wood School

The World I Would Like To Live In

Happy people, smiling everywhere they go.
The gigantic sun shining every day.
Everything is peaceful, as quiet as waves clashing at the seashore.
No rich or poor, everyone has a home.
Bullies are never seen, like wasps aren't seen in the winter.
No wars, crimes or pains are invited to this world.
Less pollution, cars run free, like bumper cars.
In this world everybody is safe.

Amy Stapleton (10)
How Wood School

The World I'd Like To Live In

The world is full of,
Lovely scented roses,
Bright pink roses like the sunset that goes down in the evening,
They smell of red strawberries, like a shining diamond,
They feel like soft, silk, furry blankets,
They blow carefully in the breeze as the wind blows gently.

The world is full of,
Glimmering diamonds,
When the sun beams down the diamonds look up to it,
They feel soft and smooth,
They roll around gently on the sand as the breeze blows calmly,
As they roll around gently, they sound like little animals walking across the world,
When they move around they leave behind them a tiny dot in the sand.

Tiffany Duran (8)
How Wood School

The World I Would Like To Live In

The world is full of lavender as purple as a parrot
The sound of robins sing in the morning on branches of blossom trees
The stones by the soothing stream as blue as the sky and as smooth as silk
Leaves on palm trees as bright as the spring grass
The sea that smells of scents of flowers crashes on the shells by the seashore
Strawberries are as red as roses
Music so soft it makes you feel sleepy.

Alicia James (9)
How Wood School

The World I Would Love To Live In

I walk into the forest and see three beautiful colours.
Sandy gold, sky-blue and cloud white.
Gold sand beneath my feet and sky-blue in the air.
Last of all, the cloud white, all in the sky.

The smell of the sea from far away
And the smell of the fresh, fresh air,
And the smell of sweet cookies in the air.

Then I see under the chair
My bracelet and my watch
That I have been trying to find all day.

Finally, I see a signpost pointing to the south.
It leads to another point in the forest.

Charlotte Cooper (9)
How Wood School

The World I Would Like To Live In

The world is full of soft music
The sound of a harp that plays softly
Like you have never heard before
The sound of a drum beating in the background
Like a beat in the clear blue sky, breezy air

The world is full of shining spring water
When the waves crash against the rocks, it makes a crashing sound
When the water comes in it pulls you and the sand out into the wavy sea
The taste of salty water when you play on your bodyboard and fall into the water

This is a beautiful life.

Victoria Wiltshire-Hersey (9)
How Wood School

The World I Would Like To Live In

As I am strolling through a misty place
I hear a poor little kitten miaowing
As I am strolling through a misty place
I see a bright, cheeky red colour floating in mid-air
As I am strolling through a misty place
I smell fresh lamb with mint sauce coming from a butcher
As I am strolling through a misty place
I see a rosy-pink colour fluttering over my head
As I am strolling through a misty place
I hear a man singing
As I am strolling through a misty place
I smell rich chocolate coming out of a local shop
As I am strolling through a misty place
I hear a howl of a grey wolf
As I am strolling through a misty place
I see a diamond rolling on the ground
As I am strolling through a misty place
I see an arrow pointing home.

Tia Smith (9)
How Wood School

The World I Would Like To Live In

I see a light blue sky above my head
The sun is fiery-red and orange
I see the sea, sea-green
I hear the wind flowing past me
I hear the drums playing loudly
I hear the trumpet playing a great tune
I see a bright diamond
I see a football waiting to be kicked in a goal.

Charlie Hyde (9)
How Wood School

The World I Would Like To Live In

I see blue as the summer sky.
I see the colour that is everywhere,
Orange as thick as a dictionary.
The last, but not least, gold.
I shine with its power and glaze.

I hear bells ringing from cells underneath the ground.
On the beach in the corner, there is a boy with two maracas.
I go to sleep when I hear the sound of jazz.

I stand near a café smelling strawberries
And pancakes with honey on,
Also orange juice with cold ice.

There are no schools and nearly 100 treasure chests.
At the end of the road there is a sign
Pointing to every kid's dream.

Adam Robbitts (9)
How Wood School

The World I Would Like To Live In

There is a grass-green just there and a sea-blue.
I hear the sound of banging drums
And see a fossil on the ground.
I smell the smell of frying chips.
I see a shining yellow and hear a ringing bell.
A howling wind blows me.
I smell a warm cup of tea.
There is a strange book showing me skyscrapers.
I hear the chimes of more bells
And smell the scent of roses.
On the road ahead, a sign
Pointing to a cave with food and water.

Tom Wernham (9)
How Wood School

The World I Would Like To Live In

As I gaze across the grey ground
I hear a jazzy sound,
The saxophone is playing loud.

As I walk on again,
These three colours pop in front of me,
A sunshine-yellow,
The pale and drowsy orange that makes you want to go to sleep
And the ruby-red that stares at me.

I see these objects in front of me,
A sparkly diamond that twinkles in the sun
And the teddy bear that I've had nearly all my life.

As I walk more and more,
I find a signpost pointing to my house
And my family is waiting there to greet me.

India Kaur-Brown (9)
How Wood School

The World I Would Like To Live In

The world is full of waves crashing and splashing down.
The dark blue, stony sea dragging back the rocks of sand,
As it goes down and splatting up,
The swirling sea going up.

The world is full of instruments,
Making lovely sounds the sun shines down by itself,
As I play the violin,
The drums banging down on the drummer,
What else could you want?

Ben Harrington (8)
How Wood School

The Nightmare

A little girl who had a little dog
That was me
A wolf chased me through dark woods
To his den.

He threw me on the floor
I didn't like it there
My dog tried to fight him
And tried to save me.

He couldn't save me
He barked and ran away
I was alone with the wolves
And that was the end of me.

Jemima Brennan (7)
Northaw School

My Otter

Black and white
As it launches into the water.
Steady and unhurried
As it rushes past.

Wet and soaked
As it washes itself with a shake and a shiver,
Its squeaky high-pitched voice tells you it's cold
And waiting to dry.

With its black long tail
It's charming to the females,
Using its whiskers
To sense its prey.

Jake Reid (10)
Northaw School

My Otter

Smooth and thin
As he glides through the water,
Charming to females
As he swims in the depths.

Soaking wet
As if from a shower,
Shakes and shivers
As he waits to dry.

Startling and squeaky
As he talks to his friends.
He uses his whiskers
To sense his prey.

George Andreou (10)
Northaw School

My Dog Dave

Dave is a cute dog,
He is very fluffy
And he is very noisy,
That's my dog Dave.

Dave is a disobedient dog,
He is bouncy and funny,
But he is very silly,
That's my dog Dave.

Dave is a playful dog,
He always barks at everything,
That's my dog Dave.

Lucy Blackwood (10)
Northaw School

My Dinosaur

My dinosaur is as big as a skyscraper,
My dinosaur is as fast as a motorbike,
My dinosaur is as tall as a plane,
My dinosaur isn't afraid.

My dinosaur is as strong as a shield,
My dinosaur is like the ocean,
My dinosaur is as calm as the wind,
My dinosaur is nice to me.

My dinosaur is as heavy as a house,
My dinosaur has the sharpest teeth,
My dinosaur is as good as God,
My dinosaur is the best to me.

Constantine Odyssea (9)
Northaw School

Charlie

Charlie is a bouncy dog
and very, very obedient.
In the park he chases frogs
and when we call him he rarely comes back.

He likes sleeping,
though wakes up at 7am in the morning.
He is sometimes quite annoying,
still very playful.

He is fluffy and cute,
minute but fast,
and when I take him on a walk
he pulls on the lead.

Emily Allen (10)
Northaw School

That's My Cat, The Daphne One

Daphne my cat is rather special,
She's not like normal cats in the street,
She likes to sleep in boxes
And bags,
That's my cat, the Daphne one!

Daphne my cat is rather lazy,
She sleeps all day and goes out at night,
She is noisy in the mornings
On a Saturday and Sunday, November,
On the piano,
That's my cat, the Daphne one!

Daphne my cat is rather cute,
With her huge blue eyes,
Just makes you want to stroke her,
That's my cat, the Daphne one!

Lily Gale (9)
Northaw School

My Dog Lilly

My dog Lilly is fluffy and rough,
She loves to play with me.
Lilly is as smooth as a duvet
And as loud as any hound could be.

Lilly is as springy as could be,
She leaps a lot, she is also very fast,
But she can be clever and playful too,
That's my good dog Lilly.

Lilly is silky as a piece of silk,
She barks like mad and Lilly is a heroine.
She is also very brave
And I love her very much.

Charlotte Lane (10)
Northaw School

Leopard Gecko

Strikes from behind rocks
Creeps from the sand
Slithers on rocks
Scaly but friendly.

Pointed head
Puffed tail
Worms and crickets are his prey
Camouflage to sand and leaves
As he gets smaller he gets darker and darker.

Prey to hawks and monitors
Food is stored in tail
Stays in one spot to hide
With yellow and black dots it's amazing to watch.

Female gecko lays eggs of two
Eyes of a different range of colour
With ears of holes in their heads.

Sean Hindes (10)
Northaw School

My Dog

My dog is very fast.
My dog is as black as a pillow.
My dog is so playful to people.
My dog isn't shy to people.
My dog is very cute.

Luke Andraé Cove (9)
Northaw School

The Bat

The bat that only comes out at night
So that it can give you a fright
As small as a mammoth
As big as a rat
Wings the size of a plane

It swoops down to the road
And hangs on a sign
Upside down and goes to sleep
But just for the day.

Then the next night comes
The bat comes out again
But this time he has his friends
They all swoop and scatter out
All around the road until they all go to a sign
And sleep through the day.

Harry Lawton (10)
Northaw School

The Sabre-Tooth Tiger

The sabre-tooth tiger is stalking its prey,
Creeping in the shadows,
His prey is hiding in the shallows.

The sabre-tooth tiger is eyeing its prey,
Staring at it straight in the eye,
'You're going down bye-bye.'

The sabre-tooth tiger is pouncing on its prey,
'This time I've got you!'
So you fall like the other two.

Ben Hardy (9)
Northaw School

My Cat Puss

Like a tiger stalking its prey
Pouncing, leaping, scurrying through bushes
And brings the prey into the house
My cat Puss.

She has huge marble eyes
As if to say 'please love me'
Her fox-like tail is so giant
That it curls round me when I cuddle her
My cat Puss.

She is like a pillow or a cuddly toy
Ginger, tabby as can be
I love her and she loves me
My cat Puss.

Nichola Few (10)
Northaw School

Profound The Rat

Big and hairy but not scary
Pinpoint every sound
Too slick to make a squeak
Eep! Make it go beep.

Going up pipes
Down tubes
As fast as a rocket
To the moon.

Climbing through the loo
To scare the person cleaning his shoes
I'm the rat that terrifies.

Henry Evans (10)
Northaw School

Flying Footballs

Once I had a dream
That I was in a football stadium,
I met all the football players.
While they were playing
I looked in the sky,
Footballs came out of nowhere.
Suddenly the football hit me on the head,
I got knocked out at 5-5.30pm.
I woke up in bed,
I had a sore head,
Then I thought it wasn't a dream.

Jonathan Hopkins (8)
Northaw School

The Killer

I went to sleep in my bed
And there I saw a head
But then I turned and there it was,
A skeleton in the Wellington
And then I saw a vampire
And then it pounced right on my face
And I was no more
But then I woke up on the floor,
I had a bad dream.

Alfie Richardson (8)
Northaw School

My Horse Piggy

Piggy is my horse
She's fast, fun and friendly.
Her coat's like a spotty dog,
Oh, that's my horse Piggy.

I love Piggy to bits
As she shows off her shiny shimmering coat
When she speeds through the fields,
Oh, that's my horse Piggy.

As she jumps in the air
She's a soaring bird floating in the sky,
For her mane is like a frantic waving hand,
Oh, that's my horse Piggy.

When the moon comes by
Piggy whinnies gently like a wolf to say goodnight,
Still excited and energetic,
She quietly goes to sleep.

Ellen Richardson (10)
Northaw School

Max

Max is cute like a puppy getting excited,
He eats chicken bones like a growling bear.

He is rapid like a cheetah flying over the plains,
He gets excited like a jumping jack.

Max catches his prey like a spiteful lion,
When he lays down he is as soft as a tiger.

He barks as loud as a lion eating someone,
Max has sharp teeth like a dinosaur.

Max is cute like a puppy getting excited,
He eats chicken bones like a growling bear.

Mattie Kyriakou (10)
Northaw School

The Poor Horse

Poor, poor horse all alone,
Living sadly without a home.
Poor, poor horse walks about,
Poor, poor horse drinking rainwater from an old dirty spout.
Poor, poor horse freezing cold,
God still loves him although he is old.
Poor, poor horse all muddy,
Poor, poor horse has lost his best friend Buddy.

Madison Rose McMahon (9)
Northaw School

My Strangest Dream

I had the strangest dream one night
Of wild bears wearing pairs of tights
And monkeys laughing like little cats,
Elephants dancing and wearing hats,
Everything was surrounding me
Even the dog drinking a cup of tea.

I hope I never have that dream again.

Sophia Constantinou (8)
Northaw School

The Amazing Dog

My dog jumps over logs,
My dog chases his tail in circles,
My dog makes my friends laugh
And we all play with him.
My dog goes on walks in the woods,
But my dog was only in my dream!
My mum would not let me have one.

Hannah Fitz-Costa (7)
Northaw School

Glowing Eyes

Eyes glowing like a cat,
The frog chased after the fly,
It leapt, it jumped,
It swam, it dived,
Spyfull in its chase.

The frog is green and black, scaly and weird,
It goes in the water and turns into things,
The frog has a spotty pattern,
Also as wet and noisy as any frog can be,
It flips, it flops, it darts, it dashes, playful in its ways.

Demitria Demosthenous (9)
Northaw School

Iggy

Iggy loves to eat, she likes to sleep
She likes to have fun all night long
My cat Iggy, she is the one.

She runs like the light in the sky
And she catches stars with no trouble at all,
She is the one.

Pouncing in and out, jumping up and down,
Twitching at any movement,
She is the one.

Max Moores (10)
Northaw School

No School

One day I walked down the road,
In the school's place I saw a *toad!*
It wasn't too big, it wasn't too small,
But then it ate the whole school hall
And then it turned to face the sun,
But then it went and knocked Class 1,
It hopped onto Class 2
And down the field the classroom flew
And while it did I sang, 'Hooray!
There will be no school today.'

Adam Lee (8)
Northaw School

My Wish

I dreamed I was in a field filled with flowers
I was making a daisy chain
I could hear deer playing
And a rabbit bouncing
Boing, boing, boing.

My friends came to join me
We played catch in the field of flowers
With a rainbow over our heads
I wish every day was like this
Then my dream would come true.

Indigo Mastroianni (8)
Northaw School

Firework Night

Fireworks, fireworks in the sky
I saw all the fireworks
And I was that guy.

I was enjoying the fireworks
But suddenly I fell
With an enormous jerk.

I hit the ground and it hurt.
I woke up with a shock
Dressed in a midnight shirt.

Beau McMahon (7)
Northaw School

My Dreams

On this day I had a dream
That I was taken
Away by aliens from space.

They took me to Jupiter
I saw clouds and the sun
And blue sky.

The stars were moving
And circling the world
As I went up.

Callum Reid (7)
Northaw School

On Land

In a land far away stood a little tree
An Ellie tree
Elephants ate it for treats
The tree was so sad
Elephants kept on eating it.

As time flew by she grew
But one day she grew some silver bells
When the elephants came near her
She rang her bells
And they all ran away.

Chloe Leonard (7)
Northaw School

My Dream

Footballs fell from the sky
Bouncing on houses
Waking people up

Children excited
Ran into the streets
Kicking footballs around

Dogs chewed bouncing cats
As the children played catch
The day footballs fell from the sky.

Arnold Bass (9)
Northaw School

Christmas

C hristmas is a snowy day,
H olly will make it great.
R udolph will guide the way,
I hope he isn't late.
S anta rides through the night,
T ime and time again.
M erry Christmas with a fright
A nd I'll see you all again.
S anta will finally have a rest!

Max Brendish (10)
Oaklands Primary School

Kittens

K ittens like to play about
I n the shed or on your head
T hey try to drink from the water spout
T hey also pretend that they're dead
E scape the house at night
N ice to have a midnight fright
S ometimes they even play fight.

Jamie Kempster (9)
Oaklands Primary School

Gazelle

G azelles jump
A t the speed of light
Z ip through grass
E longated
L uxuriantly
L ong
E legant animal.

Sam Curtis
Oaklands Primary School

Liverpool

L iverpool rule
I ncredible goal!
V ice is Carragher
E verton suck!
R ock it up, crowd
P ennant scores
O ver for Spurs
O verall, Liverpool rule
L osers, Man U!

Adam Webster (9)
Oaklands Primary School

Hallowe'en

H aving fun in the dark
A spooky time to play
L ovely decorations in the house
L aughing at the costumes
O ff the lights go
W e are having so much fun
E njoying making pumpkin faces
E ating all the sweets
N ew decorations and costumes.

Sophie Goodison (9)
Oaklands Primary School

Benson

B enson is my dog
E very day playing with his log
N aughty but nice
S ometimes watching mice
O n his bed snoring away
N ight-night Benson, see you the next day!

Sarah Cox (10)
Oaklands Primary School

My Pet Guinea Pig

My pet guinea pig runs in its wheel
And when it's very hungry it begs for a meal.
He runs up his ladder
And seems to get madder.
I love him lots
With all my dots.
But now it's dark
And so is the park.
My guinea pig is asleep, tucked in straw,
I walk away and shut the door.

Naomi Baycroft (8)
Oaklands Primary School

Fireworks

Fireworks in the sky
Zooming up so high
The colours are so bright
They are always up in flight.

Fireworks are the best
Afterwards have a rest
Don't go out with your cat
Keep it inside on the mat.

Amanveer Benning (10)
Oaklands Primary School

Football

Football is the best,
Better than the rest,
Steven Gerrard scores the goals,
Jamie Carragher plays his role,
The Kop start chanting here and there,
Watching the game is Tony Blair.

Vishva Naik (10)
Oaklands Primary School

My Little Sister

My sister picks her nose,
Then she chews her toes.
She really wants a dog,
But I think she looks like a frog.
She is really skinny,
To her the people in her class are mini.
She is seven years old,
In her room it is cold.
She has blonde hair
That looks like a bear,
So that is my little sister.

Laura Goodacre (9)
Oaklands Primary School

Dragon

Flames spitting in the sky
Hypnotic look in the eye
Different colours, different shapes
Standing out on the capes
Never go out with just a mere weapon
Or you may be lunch for the almighty dragon!

Caleb Thompson (10)
Oaklands Primary School

The Four Seasons

Winter as cold as ice
Spring, animals wake up like mice
Summer, bees come out to play
Autumn, squirrels collect their nuts for the day.

Hannah Young (10)
Oaklands Primary School

My Adventure

Here I am with no delay,
This is what I want to say,
My favourite number is twenty-four,
I can tell you'll be a bit of a bore,
Come on, shout out loud,
You can speak without a sound,
I went to the sweet shop to buy a ladder,
The service made me madder and madder,
I sat on a purple spiky bush,
Then it told me to shush,
I ran back home without delay,
That was all I wanted to say!

Beth Kendle (10)
Oaklands Primary School

What's The World Coming To?

I looked out of the window
And saw a pink lady
And a blue dog.
I looked out of the door
And saw a bright yellow fox
And a multicoloured bunny.
What's the world coming to?
I looked into the mirror
And saw a monster.
I took a pound coin
And did a runner!

Jessica Hall (9)
Oaklands Primary School

The Lion

T he razor-sharp claws
H airy golden mane
E veryone fears the opening of his jaws

L ying around preparing to pounce
I nserting fright
O ver the jungle in every single pounce
N ever losing anyone in sight.

Daniel Hughes (11)
Oaklands Primary School

What Am I?

Night hunter
Nest builder
Midnight flyer
Mouse killer.

Benjamin Davey (9)
Oaklands Primary School

My Funny Food

As sweet as sugar
As sour as a lime
My green gummy bear
Is costing me a dime.

As sticky as the tape
As gooey as melted cheese
My tomato ketchup
Is going in my tea.

Rhian Mather (11)
Oaklands Primary School

Lizards And Dragons

L izard, a scaled beast
I n the sun soaking in heat
Z oo is no place for the creature
A nimal at its best with brilliant features
R ed blood round its mouth
D ead corpses round its territory.

D ragons roaring through the sky
R ed bodies lay on the floor
A renas of blood-filled fights
G rass torn up and flying
O ver the valley dragons melting snow
N o limits to their physical strength
S o beware of the scaly scoundrels, beware.

Harvey Turner (10)
Oaklands Primary School

Best Friends

B est friends are the best
E very day they're playing out
S ometimes they even fall out
T ogether forever

F riends, friends, friends
R iding on their horses
I nvisible games too
E njoying partying
N ever neglecting
D elorice, Niamh and Naomi sharing games and having fun
S haring with our best friends.

Niamh Whicher (8)
Oaklands Primary School

Christmas!

C hristmas is a joyful time
H olly will make it fine,
R udolph will land on the roof,
I hope it's waterproof,
S ilence all through the night,
T ime to have a snowball fight,
M erry Christmas to everyone
A nd don't forget to have fun,
S uddenly Santa will give presents.

Harry Ironton (10)
Oaklands Primary School

Elephant

E lephants are great and big
L ying around being a pig
E lephants have a long trunk
P retend to be drunk
H aving a laugh
A nd with her baby calf
N aughty elephants splashing water
T hinking they're getting shorter.

Elizabeth Spear (10)
Oaklands Primary School

Cromer

C romer is the best,
R unning to the beach,
O ctopuses live in the west,
M oonlight is as round as a peach,
E arly in the morning is a fresh start,
R hyming is what teachers teach.

Emily Tomlinson (10)
Oaklands Primary School

My Complicated Day

When I woke up I had no pyjamas,
I went downstairs,
I found my breakfast and ate thin air.
I went to school without moving.
At school I did lots of writing without picking up a pen.
At lunchtime I had a delicious lunch but didn't eat it.
When I went home and went in but did not open the door.
I went swimming and left my swimming trunks at home.
When I got in the swimming pool I drowned
In a pool with no water in it!
I woke up from the dead and started all over again.

Tamara Fajinmi (9)
Oaklands Primary School

The Undercover Riders

John Rider, he's always a flyer,
His son Alex Rider he is never a crier.
Ian Rider, he's an undercover agent,
Alex's mum and dad died in a plane crash.
Jack Starbright is Alex's carer, she always cooks things in
under 5 minutes.
So that's the Ryder family, you won't understand anymore than I do!

Sulaimaan Mughal (10)
Oaklands Primary School

Zombies

Z ombies, zombies, axe in the head
O ut of the grave and into your bed
M ounts an axe in your head, bound to make you squeal
B rains, brains, squishy and squelchy, what a brilliant meal
I n the grave dwelling now
E xtremely strong they will get
S o everyone is in danger, you had better run!

James Curtis (10)
Oaklands Primary School

Beware!

There dwelt in a cave
A savage, monstrous beast
Who dined on human and animal flesh
To eat as a feast.

More vicious than a manticore
With a gruesome head of a Minotaur.
Poisonous snakes in its writhing hair
And gruesome claws that tear.

A staring eye, a basilisk,
The freakish wings of a hippogriff,
Fiendish mind of a goblin,
Yellow teeth as sharp as pins.

Devours humans, big and small,
Whether they are short or tall.
It swallows them completely whole,
Heedless of plate or bowl.

So when you happen to go this way,
The way of the mountain pass,
Make sure you travel during the day
Or beware the gruesome wrath . . .
Beware!

Emily Beswick (11)
Oaklands Primary School

Puppies

P uppies are cuddly and sweet
U p and jolly puppies are so sweet
P uppies are so cute
P eople love puppies
I love puppies so much
E ven though they can bite
S trawberries are sweet but not as sweet as puppies.

Megan Jackson (8)
Oaklands Primary School

The Grim Reaper

His face is dark
It may be a laugh
But his claws are vicious
And his axe is sharp.

He follows you everywhere
Either Egypt or Iraq
You see the sign of death
And next an axe in your back.

When you don't know he's there
He stares at you as you lie
You wake up in the morning
Screaming, 'I don't want to die.'

It's the day of Hallowe'en
And everyone is scared
Everyone won't be killed
But the world was suddenly teared.

Ha, ha, ha!

Joshua James Heyman (10)
Oaklands Primary School

Genie In A Bottle

If I found a genie in a bottle
And then I had three wishes,
My first would be to make my mum
Always do the dishes.

My second would be
To have some girl chasing me around
For an autograph that I will give,
But only when I'm found.

My third would be to have some cash
And always chips for tea,
That is what I wish, so
I need genies to come visit me!

James Firth (10)
Oaklands Primary School

A Dream In Bed

A sleep in my bed at night

D reaming of a flying carpet
R oaming in the skies
E verything calm and peaceful
A sight is there to see
M orning time has come and the sun arises

I mpossible, the sun turns red and yellow
N o, orange and pink, an amazing view

B eyond anything ever seen
E very day I wish I could see that
D eep memories of it will never go . . .

Lucy Reynolds (10)
Oaklands Primary School

Hallowe'en

Hallowe'en is near
So you might start to hear
Goblins creeping about in the night
Or a wizard could give you a fright
A witch could cast a spell on you
And you probably won't know what to do
People will knock on your door
Wanting candy more and more
People will be scaring you
They might make you want to go to the loo
Hallowe'en is getting near
So you want to stay clear!

Rhianne Batty
Oaklands Primary School

Snakes

S nakes slither slyly looking for food
N ot even a mouse knows when it's going to pop out
A gigantic snake, slithering like a long ladder
K iller snake clawing its prey and blinding it
E normous snakes slithering up trees to find insects
S nakes are the best ever!

Renée Beane (8)
Oaklands Primary School

The Seasons

Snow sleeps on the dead trees,
Which lay beside the warm, calm houses.
Smoke storms its way out of the rippled chimney, burnt to a crisp.
Everything that surrounds you is solid crystal white.

Spring chicks surround their mothers in happiness and joy.
The rivers and lakes begin to melt from the coldness of the
previous seasons.
Trees start to unwind and come back to life.

The sun beats down on hundreds of happy children,
Screaming at the cool midday sea.
Lush green seaweed streams into children's creations
Like mould forming around a huge castle.

Leaves begin to look as if they are being burnt in the struggling sun
Trying to fight its way through the dark clouds that are covering
the sky.

You can't even see the ground -
Leaves have invaded.

Jack Murphy (10)
St Joseph's Catholic Primary School, Waltham Cross

My Dog

My dog loves to run and play
He also listens when I say lay

My dog loves to jump and leap
And once he's finished he will go to sleep

My dog loves his walk
Sometimes on the way he will stop and talk

My dog loves his food
But he won't eat it when he's in a mood

My dog loves to go outside
But he's not allowed down my slide

My dog loves to bark
Especially at my postman mark

My dog loves his milk and water
Although he only drinks a quarter

My dog loves the car
He also likes golf but he never gets par

My dog likes his vet
But he didn't when they first met

My dog loves his Kerry
But she is married to a man called Terry

My dog loves my nan
He is her number one fan

My dog is the best
He is better than the rest.

Tommy O'Leary (11)
St Joseph's Catholic Primary School, Waltham Cross

India

The blazing hot sun beating down on me,
The sparkling crystal-blue sea in the distance,
The rich, golden sand tickling my toes.
I could smell the smoky sizzle of rice and meat
Being cooked in a little old hut.

People riding their thin glossy bikes
Down the sandy light black road.
The palm trees swaying through the mystical open air.
The taste of coconut juice out of the coconut
Makes me feel relaxed from my head to my toes.

The food is like Heaven and paradise,
All the spices roll in my mouth,
I can really taste the flavour and the texture,
It's like I am in my own little world,
Everywhere you go is amazing,
The people greet you like you're part of them.

Clothes made with the finest silk,
The colours are rare but not to India.
Satin, emerald, ruby, all there,
Diamonds, pearls, rubies, they're everywhere.
It is a memory I will never forget.

Sadira Patrick (10)
St Joseph's Catholic Primary School, Waltham Cross

Sunny Day

Today is a sunny day when the clouds are not in sight,
The birds are singing in the trees and there is a wonderful sight.
The summer sun is blazing, straight down from the clear blue sky,
The flowers are blooming like little gems every shape and size.
The lake is glistening like the morning sun coming up from the mountainside,
While I rest my head and go to sleep, that's all for now . . .

Jessica Lipani (11)
St Joseph's Catholic Primary School, Waltham Cross

Hallowe'en

The pumpkins chuckle as the moon awakes,
The trolls stomp their feet to cause earthquakes!

The Hallowe'en costumes fly onto a broom,
The witch finds out and gets furious soon!

The apples queue up to be smothered in toffee,
As the scones get in line to be eaten with coffee!

A freaky Frankenstein chases Scooby-Doo
And the spooky ornaments stare intently at you!

Bats can't help themselves but they have to stop and think,
Before they cover the room in toffee as quick as a wink!

Dracula sucks treacle instead of blood,
Cos the closest he can find is gummy worms and chocolate mud!

Skeletons bump into things and every time they do,
They create havoc in every room too!

Mary O'Driscoll (10)
St Joseph's Catholic Primary School, Waltham Cross

My Christmas Tree

I love my bright green Christmas tree,
Underneath are lots of presents for me.
It glimmers, sparkles and shimmers all night,
It is wrapped with tiny fairy lights.
An angel perches high on top
Among sweet-smelling needles that should not drop.
Coated in tinsel all shiny and new,
Red, gold, silver and blue.
With bright shiny baubles and gingerbread men,
It is time to celebrate Christmas again.

Georgia Matthews (10)
St Joseph's Catholic Primary School, Waltham Cross

The Big Match

Today's the day
The day of the big game
The shirts we wear may be different
But our dreams are the same.

Both teams want the cup
It's all about the silverware
Our hearts want it so much
I can see this game isn't going to be fair.

The whistle blows
The first half begins
Both teams defend and attack down the wings.

Not many chances are created
Both teams are even
Neither one of these teams will give up and be beaten.

So on to the second half the match goes
What will be the outcome?
Nobody knows.

During the second half the momentum isn't the same
Everything is faster
In this great game.

The striker shoots
His shot soars
Right into the top corner
The striker scores.

The final whistle blows
The winners celebrate
The losers confidence is down
Until someone shouts, 'There's always next break.'

James Deady (11)
St Joseph's Catholic Primary School, Waltham Cross

My Friends

My friends are always there for me,
They help me through my troubles
No matter what they may be.

Whether I'm sad or glad,
They will be there,
We always have lots of secrets to share.

Good friends are very kind,
Especially those who have others in mind.

In happiness and laughter,
In sadness and tears,
Thanks to all my friends
I will overcome my fears.

Daniel Spagnuolo (10)
St Joseph's Catholic Primary School, Waltham Cross

Corsica Dreams

Corsica has a great view,
I'd recommend it for you!
A radiant sky and a deep blue sea,
Everyone's smiling with glee!
From the Mediterranean, a bluey-green,
On the horizon a boat is seen.
The elegant white boat came into bay,
The beach leads to a stone pathway.
The pathway comes to a cottage small,
With two blue shutters and a white wall.
The bushes tame and the grass grown wild,
Out the cottage comes an excited child!
Corsica, the Mediterranean jewel!
My Corsica dreams are really cool!

Sean O'Driscoll (10)
St Joseph's Catholic Primary School, Waltham Cross

The War And Me

It's so cold,
No one to hold,
No one to ask why it's so cold.

I don't know what to do,
I really want to hold my teddy bear Sue.
You don't know what I feel like,
I feel so sorry for my little brother Mike.

I'm starting to feel a little sick,
My annoyed mother gave me a flick.
She is going red with stress
As our hide-out is a mess.

The damp is getting me down,
I'm starting to form a frown.
The bombs are getting bad,
They're making everyone sad.

The Germans make me feel weak
Because of the danger that they seek.
My dad has just passed away,
I miss him every day.

I want to run away,
To somewhere where I can stay.
I want the war to end,
As it's driving me around the bend.

Lola Carrington (10)
St Joseph's Catholic Primary School, Waltham Cross

Mission Complete

The spy crept into the room,
Everybody was silent but then he heard *boom!*
An explosion had just gone off,
But the spy walked away with only a minor cough,
He ignored it and just went on like he was running a marathon.
He looked in the hallway, he looked twice,
Even spotted some black, scruffy mice.
He then went in but, oh no!
The hallway ceiling was just too low.
He hit his head and fell to the floor,
To be captured once more.
But actually he hadn't hurt his head,
He was just pretending to be dead.
The evil henchman came up to him
And even tried to do him in,
But the spy shot him with his gun,
Payback time had just begun!
Into the main office
Where the evil boss stays, and he's called Boris!
He planted a bomb and ran for his life,
Not because he wanted to get home to his wife.
He ran out the entrance and *kaboom!*
The bomb exploded right there in the room.
He walked away from the fiery heat
And then just said, 'Mission complete!'

Callum Higgins (10)
St Joseph's Catholic Primary School, Waltham Cross

My Uncle

Football lover
Crazy driver
Loud laughter
Big eater
Plant lover
Tea drinker
Dog hater
Great gardener.

Jake Long (10)
Sandon JMI School

Spider

Fly catcher
Bath squatter
Web spinner
Mum frightener
Good runner
Little eater
Fast walker.

Jacob Kingston (9)
Sandon JMI School

My Brother

Big brother
Loud shouter
Early waker
Painful hitter
Bad kicker
Naughty creature
Messy eater.

Helen Inman (9)
Sandon JMI School

Me, Myself And I

Chocolate lover
Helpful mother
Kung-fu kicker
Hates Snickers
Loud speaker
Cake eater
Good cheater
Heavy sleeper
Beauty queen
Never mean.

Amelia Kirsty White (10)
Sandon JMI School

Me

Score snatcher
Chip scorer
Scary tackler
Leg hurter
Great footballer
Fantastic kicker
Ball hogger.

Ellis Brown (10)
Sandon JMI School

My Brother

Brilliant footballer
Loud sleeper
Rubbish dancer
Unique runner
Horrible counter
My brother.

Georgina Simpson (10)
Sandon JMI School

My Cat

Loud snorer
Big eater
Fast runner
Mirror boxer
Hair maker
Bird catcher
High jumper
Finger biter
Who am I?

Daniel Morris (10)
Sandon JMI School

Liam

Nail biter
Football striker
Arsenal lover
Cake maker
Wide grinner
Hair geler
My brother.

Chelsea Folly (9)
Sandon JMI School

Looking Out Of The Window

Looking out of the window
I saw a peaceful blue sky.
Then suddenly . . .
An aeroplane whizzed by
And disappeared straight through a fluffy white cloud.
Peace again.

Jacob Anderson (8)
Sandon JMI School

Who Am I?

Oven glove eater
Painful biter
Night barker
Playful runner
Silly dancer
Garden digger
Cat annoyer
Bed flinger
Bag chewer
Cute sleeper.

My dog.

Alice Rush (10)
Sandon JMI School

Me

Coat sucker
Hair spiker
Computer player
Dog stroker
Good sleeper
Goalie player
Pasta lover
Football lover
Star performer.

Jack Darton (9)
Sandon JMI School

Winter Poem

As the leaves touch the ground
They give the earth a crispy feel.
The ice feels so cold and the way the leaves curl up
It makes me feel freezing.

Chloe May Bland (9)
Wheatfields Junior School

Fudge

How I wish of a world of fudge,
Soft but chewy,
My favourite treat.

Whenever I get the chance
I slowly suck,
Trying to make the pleasure last forever.

I love the feeling of the fudge
Sticking to my teeth,
I can't resist,
I need it now.

I sneak silently to the cupboard,
I sniff the air,
Oh yes, it is there,
My favourite smell,
Wafting in the air,
I take a careful bite,
The sound of victory,
Melting in my mouth.

James Bromfield (7)
Wheatfields Junior School

The Best Dogs

I like dogs because they are happy and friendly.
I like all sorts of dogs,
I like thin dogs, small dogs, fat dogs and even long-legged dogs,
But most of all my favourite sort of dogs are bull mastiffs,
Boxers and sausage dogs.
If you were a dog my favourite one would be *you!*

Maizie Batham
Wheatfields Junior School

Friendship

Everyone loves friends
Playing around all day
You don't even have to pay for friends

Friends rule
They never fight
You can go to the mall with friends

You draw together
You work together
You care for each other
You're just friends

Best friends.

Emily Caswell (8)
Wheatfields Junior School

Death By Morning

In my bedroom,
About to go to bed,
When a trigger sounds behind me
And a gun's against my head,
The ice-cold barrel
Sends a shiver down my spine,
The fear in the air is definitely mine,
A darkness forms around me,
A sharp pain in my back,
My last words were, 'Don't kill me.'
Then everything went black.

Charlotte Fernandez (9)
Wheatfields Junior School

Autumn Poem

I see a clear, misty morning,
Just as the sun is dawning.
A silvery powder covers the ground
And through the air is a silent sound.
The colours of fire cover the lawn,
For every morning the world is reborn.

The trees are losing their wonderful seeds,
One jolt of the branch, that's all it needs.
As spiders spin their webs out of silk,
The dew settles, looking like crystallised milk.
This autumn pleasure doesn't lack glory,
But in a few minutes, it's the end of the story.

Kathryn Wormald (10)
Wheatfields Junior School

Hallowe'en

31st of October is Hallowe'en,
You'd better watch out or you may be seen.
Trick or treat is what you do
But be very careful who you go to.
There are lots of costumes you can wear.
Dracula, witches and even a bear.
After dark the pumpkins are lit
To keep all the spooks away or you may have a fit.

Lauren Morley-Hewson (8)
Wheatfields Junior School

Yoga

Stretch, bend, stretch, bend,
Stretch and bend,
All day long do the dog, do the cat,
Lay back and relax, be quiet,
Think you are at the seaside playing, laughing
All day long.

Stretch, bend, stretch, bend,
Stretch and bend,
All day long do the plank, do the grasshopper
Lay back and relax,
Think you are on a ship
Sailing all day long.

Stretch, bend, stretch, bend,
Stretch and bend,
All day long do the tree, do the lion
Lay back and relax,
Think you are in the jungle
Exploring all day long.

Daisy Corke (9)
Wheatfields Junior School

Scary, Hungry Hallowe'en

People in scary costumes
Running round the streets,
Not having any dinner,
Unless it includes sweets.
Costumes like witches,
Costumes like bats,
Maybe even something,
Scarier than that!

Lucy Guy (8)
Wheatfields Junior School

Fireworks, Fireworks

Fireworks, fireworks you light the sky
With sparkles so high, they drop down
But don't make much sound.
The swirls that go up are colourful and hot,
The families all stand in a safe spot.
A rocket zooms past,
The crowd all gasp!
Round and round spins the Catherine wheel
While the screamers let out an ear-piercing squeal,
Then hot dogs and cola once it is over!

Charlotte Dunkerley (7)
Wheatfields Junior School

Tiger, Tiger

T iger in the dark I hear you
I n the jungle I have found you
G o, my tiger, like the wind, you
E nchant me with your hidden power and
R oar to me across the world.

T iger in the past I heard you,
I n the future will I meet you?
G reat the threat your stripes have won you.
E ver will I strive to save you and
R oar to me across the world.

Heather McConnell (9)
Wheatfields Junior School

My Dog

You are gorgeous and fluffy
You are never ever scruffy
You are clever and bright
You always know what's right

Your dark blue eyes are your best feature
You are the one and only creature that I love
When you gaze up at me with your puppy-eyed look
I would forgive you for the sausages you took

I love to play with you all the time
Because you are all mine
I just wish you were real.

Freya Rogers (8)
Wheatfields Junior School

Five Monkeys

Five little monkeys swinging on five vines,
Their bodies are thin, just like lines.
They are praying for bananas to the banana god,
Getting bananas with a fishing rod.

Then stealing someone's banana hat,
Peeling the banana and squashing it flat.
Throwing the skin for someone to slip,
Those five little monkeys having a banana trip.

Alice Powell (7)
Wheatfields Junior School

Young Writers Information

We hope you have enjoyed reading this book - and that you will continue to enjoy it in the coming years.

If you like reading and writing poetry drop us a line, or give us a call, and we'll send you a free information pack.

Alternatively if you would like to order further copies of this book or any of our other titles, then please give us a call or log onto our website at www.youngwriters.co.uk

Young Writers Information
Remus House
Coltsfoot Drive
Peterborough
PE2 9JX

(01733) 890066